General editor: Graham Handle

Brodie's Notes on William Shakespeare's

Macbeth

Graham Handley MA PH D
Formerly Principal Lecturer and Head of English Department,
The College of All Saints, Tottenham

Pan Books London, Sydney and Auckland

First published 1985 by Pan Books Ltd,
Cavaye Place, London SW10 9PG
39 38 37 36 35
© Graham Handley 1985
ISBN 0 330 50186 0
Photoset by Parker Typesetting Service, Leicester
Printed and bound in Great Britain by
Richard Clay Ltd, Bungay, Suffolk

Other titles by Graham Handley in the Brodie's Notes series:
As You Like It
Twelfth Night

Contents

Preface by the general editor   5

Shakespeare and the Elizabethan playhouse   7

Literary terms used in these notes   11

The play   12
Plot   12
Source   13
Treatment   14
Date   15

Scene summaries, critical comment, textual notes and revision questions
Act I   16
Act II   29
Act III   38
Act IV   47
Act V   57

General questions   64

Shakespeare's art in *Macbeth*

Setting   66

Themes   66

The characters
Macbeth 67, Lady Macbeth 71, Duncan 76, Banquo 77,
Macduff 78, Malcolm 80, Minor characters 80

Style and structure
Introduction   82
Imagery and symbols 82, (Clothes 84, Sleep 85, The grave 85,
The natural and supernatural 86,
The witches 86), Verse (Couplets 87, Key words 88,
The soliloquy 89, Variety 91), Prose 92

Further reading   95

Line references in these Notes are to the
Arden Shakespeare: Macbeth,
but as references are also given
to particular acts and scenes,
the Notes may be used
with any edition of the play.

Preface

This student revision aid is based on the principle that in any close examination of Shakespeare's plays 'the text's the thing'. Seeing a performance, or listening to a tape or record of a performance, is essential and is in itself a valuable and stimulating experience in understanding and appreciation. However, a real evaluation of Shakespeare's greatness, of his universality and of the nature of his literary and dramatic art, can only be achieved by constant application to the texts of the plays themselves. These revised editions of Brodie's Notes are intended to supplement that process through detailed critical commentary.

The first aim of each book is to fix the whole play in the reader's mind by providing a concise summary of the plot, relating it back, where appropriate, to its source or sources. Subsequently the book provides a summary of each scene, followed by *critical comments*. These may convey its importance in the dramatic structure of the play, creation of atmosphere, indication of character development, significance of figurative language etc, and they will also explain or paraphrase difficult words or phrases and identify meaningful references. At the end of each act revision questions are set to test the student's specific and broad understanding and appreciation of the play.

An extended critical commentary follows this scene by scene analysis. This embraces such major elements as characterization, imagery, the use of blank verse and prose, soliloquies and other aspects of the play which the editor considers need close attention. The paramount aim is to send the reader back to the text. The book concludes with a series of revision questions which require a detailed knowledge of the play; the first of these has notes by the editor of what *might* be included in a written answer. The intention is to stimulate and to guide; the whole emphasis of this commentary is to encourage the student's *involvement* in the play, to develop disciplined critical responses and thus promote personal enrichment through the imaginative experience of our greatest writer.

Graham Handley

Shakespeare and the Elizabethan playhouse

William Shakespeare was born in Stratford-upon-Avon in 1564, and there are reasons to suppose that he came from a relatively prosperous family. He was probably educated at Stratford Grammar School and, at the age of eighteen, married Anne Hathaway, who was twenty-six. They had three children, a girl born shortly after their marriage, followed by twins in 1585 (the boy died in 1596). It seems likely that Shakespeare left for London shortly after a company of visiting players had visited Stratford in 1585, for by 1592 – according to the jealous testimony of one of his fellow-writers Robert Greene – he was certainly making his way both as actor and dramatist. The theatres were closed because of the plague in 1593; when they reopened Shakespeare worked with the Lord Chamberlain's men, later the King's men, and became a shareholder in each of the two theatres with which he was most closely associated, the Globe and the Blackfriars. He later purchased New Place, a considerable property in his home town of Stratford, to which he retired in 1611; there he entertained his great contemporary Ben Jonson (1572–1637) and the poet Michael Drayton (1563–1631). An astute businessman, Shakespeare lived comfortably in the town until his death in 1616.

This is a very brief outline of the life of our greatest writer, for little more can be said of him with certainty, though the plays – and poems – are living witness to the wisdom, humanity and many-faceted nature of the man. He was both popular and successful as a dramatist, perhaps less so as an actor. He probably began work as a dramatist in the late 1580s, by collaborating with other playwrights and adapting old plays, and by 1598 Francis Meres was paying tribute to his excellence in both comedy and tragedy. His first original play was probably *Love's Labour's Lost* (1590) and while the theatres were closed during the plague he wrote his narrative poems *Venus and Adonis* (1593) and *The Rape of Lucrece* (1594). The sonnets were almost certainly written in the 1590s, though not published until 1609; the first 126 are addressed to a young man who was his friend and patron, while the rest are concerned with the 'dark lady'.

The dating of Shakespeare's plays has exercised scholars ever since the publication of the First Folio (1623), which listed them as comedies, histories and tragedies. It seems more important to look at them chronologically as far as possible, in order to trace Shakespeare's considerable development as a dramatist. The first period, say to the middle of the 1590s, included such plays as *Love's Labour's Lost*, *The Comedy of Errors*, *Richard III*, *The Taming of the Shrew*, *Romeo and Juliet* and *Richard II*. These early plays embrace the categories listed in the First Folio, so that Shakespeare the craftsman is evident in his capacity for variety of subject and treatment. The next phase includes *A Midsummer's Night's Dream*, *The Merchant of Venice*, *Henry IV Parts 1 and 2*, *Henry V* and *Much Ado About Nothing*, as well as *Julius Caesar*, *As You Like It* and *Twelfth Night*. These are followed, in the early years of the century, by his great tragic period: *Hamlet*, *Othello*, *King Lear* and *Macbeth*, with *Antony and Cleopatra* and *Coriolanus* belonging to 1607–09. The final phase embraces the romances (1610–13), *Cymbeline*, *The Tempest* and *The Winter's Tale* and the historical play *Henry VIII*.

Each of these revision aids will place the individual text under examination in the chronology of the remarkable dramatic output that spanned twenty years from the early 1590s to about 1613. The practical theatre for which Shakespeare wrote and acted derived from the inn courtyards in which performances had taken place, the few playhouses in his day being modelled on their structure. They were circular or hexagonal in shape, allowing the balconies and boxes around the walls full view of the stage. This large stage, which had no scenery, jutted out into the pit, the most extensive part of the theatre, where the poorer people – the 'groundlings' – stood. There was no roof (though the Blackfriars, used from 1608 onwards, was an indoor theatre) and thus bad weather meant no performance. Certain plays were acted at court, and these private performances normally marked some special occasion. Costumes, often rich ones, were used, and music was a common feature, with musicians on or under the stage; this sometimes had additional features, for example a trapdoor to facilitate the entry of a ghost. Women were barred by law from appearing on stage, and all female parts were played by boy actors; this undoubtedly explains the many instances in Shakespeare where a woman has to conceal her identity by disguising herself as a man, e.g. Rosalind in *As You Like It*, Viola in *Twelfth Night*.

Shakespeare and his contemporaries often adapted their plays from sources in history and literature, extending an incident or a myth or creating a dramatic narrative from known facts. They

were always aware of their own audiences, and frequently included topical references, sometimes of a satirical flavour, which would appeal to – and be understood by – the ground-lings as well as their wealthier patrons who occupied the boxes. Shakespeare obviously learned much from his fellow dramatists and actors, being on good terms with many of them. Ben Jonson paid generous tribute to him in the lines prefaced to the First Folio of Shakespeare's plays:

Thou art a monument without a tomb,
And art alive still, while thy book doth live
And we have wits to read, and praise to give.

Among his contemporaries were Thomas Kyd (1558–94) and Christopher Marlowe (1564–93). Kyd wrote *The Spanish Tragedy*, the revenge motif here foreshadowing the much more sophis-ticated treatment evident in *Hamlet*, while Marlowe evolved the 'mighty line' of blank verse, a combination of natural speech and elevated poetry. The quality and variety of Shakespeare's blank verse owes something to the innovatory brilliance of Marlowe, but carries the stamp of individuality, richness of association, technical virtuosity and, above all, the genius of imaginative power.

The texts of Shakespeare's plays are still rich sources for scholars, and the editors of these revision aids have used the Arden editions of Shakespeare, which are regarded as pre-eminent for their scholarly approach. They are strongly recom-mended for advanced students, but other editions, like The New Penguin Shakespeare, The New Swan, The Signet are all good annotated editions currently available. A reading list of selected reliable works on the play being studied is provided at the end of each commentary and students are advised to turn to these as their interest in the play deepens.

Literary terms used in these notes

Simile A comparison between two objects that are fundamentally dissimilar. It is introduced by the words 'like' or 'as':

And Pity, like a naked new-born babe,
Striding the blast, or heaven's Cherubins, hors'd
Upon the sightless couriers of the air . . . *Macbeth* (Act I, Scene 7)

Metaphor A compressed comparison, but without the use of 'like' or 'as': His silver skin lac'd with his golden blood (Act II, Scene 3)

Personification This is when an object, something abstract or an idea, is addressed as if it had personal or human qualities:

Come, seeling Night,
Scarf up the tender eye of pitiful Day (Act III, Scene 2)

Alliteration The repetition of letters, generally at the beginning of each word, which are the same: darkness does . . . living light . . . pride of place (Act II, Scene 4)

Anachronism A reference to something which did not exist at the time the events in the play took place, i.e. the mention of 'dollars' in Act I, Scene 2.

Antithesis The balancing of two opposite ideas or expressions in the same phrase or sentence or in two parallel sentences or phrases: it makes him, and it mars him; it sets him on, and it takes him off; it persuades him, and disheartens him . . . (Act II, Scene 3)

Climax i.e. an ascending scale of ideas or of ideas conveyed in figurative language. The opposite is **anti-climax**, usually called **bathos**, where the ideas expressed are ridiculous rather than impressive.

Irony (a) where the words used imply the opposite of what they usually mean and (b) a situation in which what should be and what actually is are different.

Dramatic Irony This is where the audience understands something which a character or characters on stage do not. *Macbeth* is full of dramatic irony, witness Act II, Scene 3, the Porter's scene, where the Porter, Macduff and Lennox do not know that Duncan has been murdered.

Hyperbole Exaggeration or distortion. Sometimes in *Macbeth* this heightens the dramatic effect:

Most sacrilegious Murder hath broke ope
The Lord's anointed Temple . . .

destroy your sight
With a new Gorgon. (Act II, Scene 3)

The play
Plot

Macbeth and Banquo, Scottish generals, are returning after crushing a rebellion against Duncan, King of Scotland, when they are met by three witches; these greet Macbeth as Thane of Cawdor and King hereafter, and prophesy that Banquo shall be father to a line of kings. Shortly afterwards messengers arrive to tell Macbeth that Duncan has created him Thane of Cawdor as a reward for his services. Macbeth ponders on this, and writes the news to his wife, who determines to do all that she can to make him king. Duncan honours Macbeth further by coming to stay at his castle; there, urged on by Lady Macbeth's force and practical capacity, Macbeth murders the king. Though some suspect him, he is made King.

In view of the witches' prophecy regarding Banquo, Macbeth tries to make himself secure on the throne by hiring murderers to kill Banquo and his son Fleance; the latter escapes. Later that evening at a banquet Macbeth – and Macbeth alone – sees the ghost of the murdered Banquo sitting in his place at the table. Only the ingenuity of Lady Macbeth saves her husband from revealing his guilt to the assembled guests. Macbeth, already a tyrant, seeks out the witches, who bid him beware of Macduff. They provide him with some security by telling him that none of woman born shall harm him, and that he will never be defeated until Birnam Wood moves to Dunsinane Hill. But they also provide a show of kings, the descendants of Banquo, the coming rulers of Scotland.

Warned by the witches Macbeth determines to kill Macduff who, however, escapes; Macbeth has Macduff's wife and children murdered. Ross takes the news to Macduff, who is now in England with Malcolm, eldest son of Duncan and rightful heir to the throne of Scotland. They determine, with English aid, to overthrow Macbeth, Macduff vowing personal vengeance on the tyrant. The effects of Macbeth's murders and misrule are now seen in these forces gathering against him, and he is besieged in his castle at Dunsinane. Meanwhile Lady Macbeth, who has gone mad, takes her own life.

Malcolm tells his soldiers each to take a bough from Birnam Wood as camouflage as they advance. During the battle Macduff reveals that he was from his mother's womb 'untimely ripped'.

He fights with Macbeth and kills him; the prophecies of the witches are fulfilled, and Malcolm assumes the throne.

Source

The story of *Macbeth* is taken from Raphael Holinshed's *Chronicles of England, Scotland and Ireland* (1577), which are in his name but written by several people. The rebellion of Macdonwald is described, and it is put down by Duncan's generals, Macbeth and Banquo. Macdonwald's men desert him; he flees to a castle, kills himself, his wife and children. When Macbeth enters and finds him dead, he has Macdonwald's head put on a pole and sent to Duncan.

Meanwhile Sweno, King of Norway, arrives with a large force of men, and this is opposed by a triple army, each section being led by Duncan, Macbeth and Banquo respectively. Sweno defeats the King's army and hopes to conquer the rest of the kingdom without bloodshed. He besieges Duncan in a castle, but Duncan gets a secret message via Banquo to Macbeth, and enters into negotiations with Sweno, sending provisions for his men. These contain a juice from certain berries which induce deep sleep. Macbeth, summoned by Duncan, slaughters the drugged army, Sweno and ten others escaping.

The Scots celebrate, but Canute of England, brother of Sweno, sends a Danish fleet to avenge the defeat; Macbeth and Banquo overcome this force, Macbeth receiving a great sum of gold and the Danes burying their dead at Saint Colme's Inch. Macbeth and Banquo journey towards Forres, meet three witches who utter the prophecies about Macbeth being Thane of Glamis, Cawdor and King hereafter, as well as replying to Banquo's questions by saying that his heirs will rule Scotland for a long time, 'by continual descent'. Macbeth and Banquo joke about the prophecies, thinking that they have seen either the goddesses of destiny or some nymphs and fairies.

Macbeth is made Thane of Cawdor, Malcolm Prince of Cumberland and heir to the throne; Macbeth's wife urges him to try to gain the throne, since she is 'burning in unquenchable desire to bear the name of a queen'. Macbeth confides his ambitions to Banquo and other friends, gets their support, and kills Duncan, whose sons Malcolm and Donald Bane flee to England and Ireland respectively. Macbeth rules wisely and well in his first phase, showing 'great liberality towards the nobles of the realm', and we are told that he 'set his whole intention to maintain justice, and to punish all enormities and abuses, which had chanced through the feeble and slothful administration of Duncan'.

For ten years he rules with justice, then turns to tyranny; he has Banquo killed, but Fleance escapes. This sets him off on a chain of killings, and his greed ensures that he fills his own coffers. He has a great castle built in Dunsinane, 'the thanes of each shire in the realm' being forced to contribute to its construction. Macduff send his men to work on the castle, but won't go himself because he fears personal violence from Macbeth. Macbeth is offended and, having already been warned of Macduff by the 'three fairies or weird sisters', feels secure in the knowledge given him by 'a certain witch' that he cannot be killed by a 'man born of any woman, nor vanquished till the wood of Birnane came to the castle of Dunsinane'. Macduff begins to fear for his life and decides to enlist Malcolm's aid. Macbeth, on learning of this, goes with his men to Macduff's castle. Finding that Macduff is away, Macbeth has his wife and children slain, confiscates all his goods and has Macduff proclaimed a traitor.

In England, Macduff describes to Malcolm the pitiful state of Scotland; Malcolm, initially suspicious, and fearing that Macduff may have been 'sent from Macbeth to betray him', tests Macduff by confessing to immoderate lusts and avarice and an incapacity to govern. Macduff is anguished, and now feels 'a banished man forever' from Scotland. Malcolm reassures him, and they set about rousing the Scottish nobles.

Macbeth now fortifies Dunsinane. Arrived at Birnane Wood, Malcolm commands every soldier to 'get a bough of some tree or other'. Later Macbeth and his men flee, and Macduff pursues the tyrant. He reveals that he (Macduff) is 'even he that thy wizards have told thee of' who was 'never born of my mother, but ripped out of her womb'. He slays Macbeth, puts his head on a pole, and takes it to Malcolm; the latter assumes the throne and creates the first earls of Scotland. Macbeth's reign had lasted for seventeen years, from 1040 to 1057. Interestingly, even the detail about Old Siward's reception of his son's death is included in Holinshed.

Treatment

The above summary is intended to show just how closely *Macbeth* sticks to the outline of the story, but also to underline the subtle alterations and variations Shakespeare makes in order to concentrate dramatic effect. Throughout the Notes these changes will be evaluated in detail but some interesting departures may be noted here. Firstly, there is the combining of two battles against the rebels into one; secondly, Malcolm is named as Duncan's heir earlier, so as to give Macbeth reason for taking action quickly. Thirdly, Lady Macbeth's role is built up into a major influence in the early action, and her ambition for herself is transferred to ambition for her husband. Next, Macbeth is made host to Duncan and thus his crime against him is made all the more heinous. Banquo is represented as a man of integrity and Duncan as a good king, whereas in Holinshed it is made clear that Banquo conspired with Macbeth in the murder of Duncan, and that the latter was a villain anyway. Again the effect of the changes enhances the contrast between good and evil which runs throughout the play. Wizards and a certain witch don't appear in *Macbeth*; instead, the prophecies are confined to Macbeth's two meetings with the witches. Students should bear the summary of the source and this note on its treatment in mind as they read these Notes; it will make them more fully aware of the transforming power of Shakespeare's hand.

Date

Although this is still the subject of scholarly debate, it seems reasonably certain that *Macbeth* was written in 1605–6, and performed in 1606. Echoes in *Macbeth* of a play by Daniel and of *Sophonisba* by Marston do not seem to provide positive evidence, though certain contemporary references would support 1606. The major reference is to the Gunpowder Plot (November 1605); it has been pointed out that Shakespeare knew some of the conspirators well. The important reference occurs in the Porter's scene (Act II, Scene 3), where the porter speaks of the Jesuit priest 'who committed treason enough for God's sake, yet could not equivocate to heaven'. Father Garnet, a Jesuit, was brought to trial and hanged in 1606 for his part in the plot.

Scene summaries, critical comment, textual notes and revision questions

Act I Scene 1

Three witches in an open place; they arrange to meet again after the battle and to see Macbeth.

Commentary

This scene, though brief, sets the *supernatural* atmosphere of the play which is central to its dramatic action. The rhyming couplets give the effect of an incantation, the thunder and lightning convey the confusion of the heavens, and echo the noise of battle. 'Fair is foul' (see note below) anticipates the overturning of accepted values by unnatural acts, one of the major *themes* of the play.

three A magic number; its multiples are used significantly by the witches. (See Act I, Scene 3).

hurly burly's done When the uproar (noise of battle) is over.

lost and won A key phrase, echoed by Duncan at the end of the next scene 'What he hath lost, noble Macbeth hath won'. Ironically Duncan is to *lose* his life; Macbeth will *win* (by murder) his crown.

Graymalkin . . . Paddock Grey cat . . . toad (the witches' familiar spirits).

Anon At once.

Fair is foul 'Foul and fair' are the first words spoken in the play by Macbeth (Act I, Scene 3); the echo establishes an unconscious contact with the witches and is dramatically effective, anticipating the blurring of good and evil in Macbeth's mind.

Act I Scene 2

A Captain (Sergeant) brings news of the defeat of Macdonwald the rebel leader and his mercenaries by Macbeth, assisted by Banquo. Then the Norwegians under Sweno are also defeated and have to pay a heavy ransom, Ross telling Duncan that they were assisted by the Thane of Cawdor. The latter's title is conferred upon Macbeth by Duncan, and Ross is despatched to give Macbeth the news.

Commentary

The scene is graphic and immediate; the emphasis on blood that runs throughout the play is established. The language is vivid in description, the images (of the 'two spent swimmers', 'As sparrows, eagles, or the hare the lion') are from nature, and Macbeth is to go against what is natural. Expectation is built up about Macbeth who, from accounts of him, seems larger than life. The tragic hero must have noble qualities, and these reports of Macbeth stress his fearlessness in battle, his exultation in action: both important facets of his character.

bloody Mention of blood is frequent in *Macbeth*, its stress underlining the violence of the action.

newest state Latest news.

hardy Brave.

'Gainst my captivity i.e. in case I am taken prisoner.

knowledge of the broil State of the battle.

choke their art Make their skill (as swimmers) useless.

to that To that end or purpose.

The multiplying villainies . . . him The comparison is with lice, one of a number of bodily affliction images in *Macbeth*.

western isles The Hebrides.

Kernes and Gallowglasses Lightly and heavily armed troops.

And Fortune . . . a rebel's whore Fickle Fortune was on Macdonwald's side.

smok'd with bloody execution Heated as he killed in battle.

Valour's minion . . . the slave Bravery's favourite . . . Macdonwald.

unseam'd him from the nave to th' chops Slit him open from the navel to the jaws (the first of the tailoring or clothes images in the play).

As whence the sun . . . swells Just as storms (discomfort) come from the same source as the sun (comfort), so when we had achieved victory fresh trouble arose.

Mark Note.

skipping Lightly armed, but also 'light' in their loyalty.

surveying vantage Seizing his opportunity.

furbish'd Newly polished up with rust removed.

say sooth Speak truly.

Doubly redoubled i.e. fought even more strongly than before (but note the word-play on 'double' elsewhere, with the word carrying the idea of Macbeth 'double-crossing' Duncan).

except Unless.

memorize another Golgotha Make as memorable as Calvary (Mark 15, 22).

What a haste looks through his eyes! His eyes show that he is bursting to reveal his news.

Fife Area between the Firths of Forth and Tay.

flout . . . fan our people cold The image is used to describe the
beginning of the battle, the Norwegian banners causing fear among
the Scots.

dismal Disastrous.

Bellona's bridegroom i.e. Macbeth (Bellona was the Roman goddess of
war, wife of Mars).

lapp'd in proof Wearing tested armour.

Confronted him with self-comparisons Stood up to him, was in every
way a match for him (ironically, even to treachery).

lavish Insolent.

composition Terms to be agreed under a truce.

Saint Colme's Inch Inchcolm, the small island in the Firth of Forth.

dollars Sixteenth-century Bohemian coins, and thus an anachronism
here.

What he hath lost . . . Macbeth hath won Note the echo of the witches'
words in Scene 1, and also that *both* Thanes of Cawdor are traitors, the
one in the past, the other in the future, an ironic linking.

Act I Scene 3

The witches await Macbeth on the heath, boasting of their
powers; when he enters they greet him as Thane of Glamis
(which he is), Thane of Cawdor (which he doesn't yet know
about) and 'King hereafter'. Banquo, who is with Macbeth,
notices that he 'starts' at the prophecies, asks the witches to speak
to him, whereupon they tell him that he will be father to kings.
Macbeth urges them to tell him more but they disappear, and
shortly afterwards Ross and Angus arrive, bearing Duncan's
thanks and investing Macbeth with the title of Thane of Cawdor.
Macbeth ponders on this speedy fulfilment of the witches'
second prophecy (strictly the first since Macbeth is already
Thane of Glamis) but Banquo warns him of the treachery of
'The instruments of darkness'. Macbeth becomes 'rapt', thinking
of the 'ill' and 'good' of the prophecies, and considering that he
may even become King by 'chance'. He tells Banquo that he
would like to speak to him further about what has happened.

Commentary

The initial part of the scene is an invocation to evil; Macbeth's
first words echo the words of the witches in Scene 1, and the
prophecies and their immediate effect on Macbeth show that he
has perhaps harboured some thoughts of advancement. By contrast Banquo, though he wishes to know more, reacts openly;
when Ross tells Macbeth that he is Thane of Cawdor, Banquo

ascribes the fulfilment of the prophecy to 'the Devil'. The contrast between Macbeth and Banquo is further underlined by Banquo's reference to betrayal, and by Macbeth's already contemplating the murder of Duncan (he sees the 'horrid image' of himself doing that). This scene sets in motion the action of the tragedy; the imagery of the stage – 'happy prologues to the swelling act' – and the key imagery of clothes ('borrowed robes', 'strange garments') emphasize that Macbeth must 'act' if he is to achieve 'the imperial theme' and 'wear' the royal clothes.

killing swine Diseases of cattle were believed to be caused by witchcraft in Shakespeare's day.

'Aroynt thee . . . rump-fed ronyon Get away with you . . . pampered, scabby creature (the witch has a fine line in abuse).

master o'th' *Tiger* Captain of the ship; *Tiger* being a common name for a ship in the Elizabethan period.

like a rat without a tail Witches could take the form of any creature, but – since witches were human females – it would always lack a tail.

do Injure (the object of her malice).

wind Witches were reputed to sell winds.

the very ports they blow i.e. the winds blowing outwards from the ports prevent ships from entering them.

shipman's card Compass.

penthouse lid The eyelid.

forbid Accursed.

sev'n-nights nine times nine Again the use of the magic number, so that the sailor will suffer for 81 weeks. (See Act I, Scene 1).

peak Get thinner.

bark Ship.

pilot's Helmsman's.

Posters Speedy, frequent travellers, messengers.

Thrice to thine . . . There are three 'all hails' to both Macbeth and Banquo, and the 'nine' reference is to occur again in Act IV, Scene 1.

wound up i.e. ready to act.

foul and fair Key words in indicating the mixture of goodness and evil in the play, and indeed in Macbeth himself.

call'd Thought to be.

aught Anything.

Choppy Chapped.

start . . . fear . . . fair Obviously Macbeth has guilty thoughts and the prophecies probe them; ironically, 'fear' and 'fair' would be pronounced the same in Shakespeare's time, and this is an instance of a pun which shows the *compression* of language and meaning in the play.

fantastical i.e. of the imagination.

noble having . . . royal hope i.e. the estates of the Thane of Cawdor . . . the hope that he will become king.

rapt Absorbed in his thoughts.

seeds of time Future.

Lesser . . . greater Note the balance of opposites here which, riddles though they are, make Banquo 'lesser' than Macbeth. He only got the 'lesser' greeting too – 'Hail'.

get Beget.

imperfect i.e. incomplete, not clear.

Sinel's Macbeth's father's.

A prosperous gentleman . . . This reveals *either* that Macbeth does not know that Cawdor has assisted the rebels, *or* that he, Macbeth, is deliberately concealing his knowledge in order to find out more from the witches.

prospect Range, possibility.

owe this strange intelligence Have obtained this strange knowledge.

bubbles . . . these are of them i.e. these manifestations (the witches) are illusions.

corporal Substantial, solid.

Would I wish.

the insane root . . . reason prisoner Hemlock, or deadly nightshade, known to induce insanity.

wonders . . . praises . . . (Duncan's) amazement and admiration make it difficult to find words.

thine, or his What you should have, what he should have, a finely economical way of expressing Macbeth's own thoughts.

Nothing afeard . . . Not frightened for yourself as you killed (but 'images of death' is a phrase appropriate to Macbeth's imagination).

post with post i.e. by every messenger

earnest Promise.

addition Title.

dress . . . borrowed robes Imagery of clothes runs throughout the play, with the ironic idea that Macbeth can wear the robes of kingship but they will be 'borrowed' since they are not lawfully his.

combin'd In alliance with.

line . . . vantage Strengthens . . . opportunity.

The greatest is behind i.e. two of the three prophecies have already been fulfilled.

trusted home Believed completely.

enkindle you unto the crown Encourage you to hope to succeed Duncan.

to win us to our harm To make us go against our better nature (the words apply to Macbeth, and Banquo appears to be warning him against himself).

instruments of Darkness Agents of the Devil.

honest trifles . . . deepest consequences Gain our confidence by revealing small truths, and then betray us over something much more serious.

prologues . . . act Note the stage imagery, a favourite Shakespearian device (cf. 'All the world's a stage' of *As You Like It*) in which life is compared to a play, here with the tragic ambition that would embrace 'the imperial theme'.

soliciting Temptation.

Cannot be ill; cannot be good Note the balance again, but here there is an abrupt rhythm which shows that the balance is hard to come by as Macbeth fights with temptation.

earnest See note p.20.

Whose horrid image doth unfix my hair i.e. the picture he has of himself murdering Duncan, which makes his hair stand (from fear) on his scalp.

Against the use of nature Contrary to what I should do (he is thinking of the unnaturalness of murder).

Present fears . . . imaginings i.e. what we worry about now are much less than the fears our imagination can make for us.

My thoughts . . . i.e. I am only imagining murder so far . . .

single state Whole nature.

function . . . surmise . . . what is not The power of action is stopped by thought, and the only reality lies in thoughts of the future, my becoming king.

stir i.e. having to act.

strange garments . . . aid of use The clothes image again. Banquo is saying that new clothes have to be worn regularly before we get accustomed to them.

Time and the hour . . . roughest day The general meaning is that life goes on, and whatever is going to happen will happen.

favour Forgiveness.

wrought Upset.

things forgotten Macbeth is already lying, something that later on he is frequently forced to do.

your pains . . . registered . . . The leaf to read them I know the trouble you have taken: the metaphor is that his mind is a memorandum book where things are written down.

chanc'd happened.

The Interim having weigh'd it i.e. having considered it carefully in the interval.

Act I Scene 4

Malcolm reports to Duncan that the Thane of Cawdor is said to have died nobly; then Duncan welcomes Macbeth and Banquo in fulsome terms, praising Macbeth, then Banquo, before announcing that Malcolm (his eldest son) will be his heir. Duncan says that he will stay with Macbeth, and the latter goes ahead to tell Lady Macbeth of the proposed royal visit, meanwhile brooding on the appointment of Malcolm and indulging his own wicked thoughts.

Commentary

The noble death of a traitor is subtly contrasted with the potential actions of the living traitor who bears the same title as the dead one. Duncan's own emphasis on the trust he had built on the first Cawdor shows his open nature and his words, 'There's no art/To find the mind's construction in the face' reflects ironically on Macbeth. Macbeth's reply to Duncan's praise should be contrasted with Banquo's – Macbeth's is fulsome, Banquo's sincere and economical; the imagery of planting/harvest is ironic, since Duncan is to reap death. By making Malcolm his heir, Duncan is showing the close-knit nature of his own family, the warmth and trust of his position, while Macbeth's soliloquy, with its imagery of darkness, is redolent of evil and deception.

in commission Ordered to carry out the execution.
Nothing . . . leaving it He behaved more nobly in death than he did in life.
studied i.e. learning the part he had to play (another metaphor from a play).
ow'd Possessed.
There's no art . . . in the face There's no way of discovering (what is going on in the mind) from the face or its expression; an ironic comment, since Macbeth is to be advised by his wife to 'Look like the innocent flower/But be the serpent under 't.'
That the proportion both of thanks and payment . . . That I could have given you thanks and honours suitable to your achievements.
more . . . pay You deserve more than anything I can give you.
our duties/Are to your throne and state Ironic words, in view of what he has thought and what he is going to do.
plant thee . . . full of growing . . . The harvest is your own Natural imagery which contrasts ironically with the unnatural deeds to come.
Wanton in fulness In unrestrained measure.
drops of sorrow Tears.
establish our estate i.e. order the succession to the throne, which was not necessarily hereditary, though in practice it often continued to be.
signs of nobleness, like stars This image, reflecting Duncan's trust and gratitude, is in strong contrast to Macbeth's invocation to darkness (which conceals light and allows evil deeds).
harbinger Forerunner.
Stars . . . light . . . black and deep desires;/The eye wink at the hand See note above for comment on light and dark imagery. The eyes must not see what the hands are doing.
in his commendation I am fed I share and enjoy the praises he receives.
banquet Feast, ironically used by Shakespeare here, since the

'banquets' of the play are crisis points – Duncan being murdered after the first, the ghost of Banquo appearing to Macbeth at the second.

a peerless kinsman Macbeth is Duncan's cousin, but 'peerless' is ironic, since he proves to be unequalled in violence and unscrupulousness.

Act I Scene 5

Lady Macbeth reading Macbeth's letter about the witches' prophecies, expresses her feeling that her husband has too much natural weakness to gain the throne. She analyses his character (see notes below) and emphasizes that she will urge him to action. When the messenger enters to tell her that Duncan is coming to stay at the castle, Lady Macbeth, at first off guard, recovers to give full rein to her own murderous thoughts, greeting Macbeth exultantly when he appears and urging him to let her undertake everything, since Duncan 'Must be provided for'.

Commentary

Macbeth's letter (in prose, a kind of unobtrusive realism on Shakespeare's part) reflects his own reaction to the witches as well as giving Lady Macbeth the news, and it provokes in her an immediate reaction – positive and forthright. Her own character, and her assessment of her husband's, is shown in her first speech: full of ambition (for him) and courage to act, a determination to bring him to the act (of murder) which his weakness would not let him undertake without 'the valour of my tongue'. Her second speech, with its invocation to evil, the wish to be freed from emotion or conscience, is startling in the violence of its language and the uncompromising murderous intention. The imagery is comparable to Macbeth's (the need for darkness) and the language itself anticipates the murder. Macbeth, man of action in battle, seems overwhelmed by his wife's directness, her counselling him to be devious, her assumption of responsibility. The dramatic temperature rises at once; we feel the tension, the imminence of violence.

The day of success i.e. the winning of the battle.
the perfect'st report Macbeth's own knowledge (i.e. the coming true of the prophecy that greeted him as Thane of Cawdor).
missives Messengers.
to deliver thee i.e. to tell you.

fear i.e. doubt.

milk of human kindness Soft and squeamish.

illness should attend it i.e. the evil that should go with it (ambition).

thou 'ldst have . . . should be undone You'd have something which can only be achieved by an act you fear to do, but if somebody else did the deed you would accept it and reap the benefits of it.

pour my spirits i.e. influence you with my passionate desire (for the murder).

chastise with the valour of my tongue Browbeat you (into action) through my brave words.

golden round i.e. the crown.

metaphysical i.e. supernatural (through the agency of the witches).

Thou art mad to say it Lady Macbeth, thinking murderous thoughts, unconsciously reveals by this phrase what has been going through her mind.

inform'd for preparation i.e. given orders to prepare (for Duncan's stay).

had the speed of Went faster than, overtook.

The raven himself is hoarse The raven is a bird of ill-omen, of impending death, the image in Lady Macbeth's mind of hoarseness being the first of the 'hard' invocations in this speech which will enable her to carry through the murder without any womanly weakness.

mortal thoughts Deadly designs.

unsex i.e. remove any weaknesses thought to belong to a woman.

make thick my blood i.e. so that no compassion can run through her veins and enter her heart.

compunctious visitings of Nature Natural feelings of pity.

fell Murderous.

nor keep peace between/Th' effect and it Nor restrain me from my object and the achievement of it.

take my milk for gall Infect my milk with bitterness.

murdering ministers Evil spirits.

sightless i.e. invisible.

You wait on Nature's mischief Attend on, wait for, unnatural happenings or occurrences.

pall An appropriate image. The pall, which is black, goes over the coffin.

the blanket of the dark A brilliantly evocative anticipation of Duncan's being murdered in bed – a dark deed concealed by the blanket of deception.

Hold Stop.

the all-hail hereafter i.e. the third prophecy of the witches, whereby Macbeth would become King in the future.

The future in the instant The coming honours at the present time.

O! never/Shall sun . . . see Lady Macbeth's determination is made clear even in this brief phrase, which suggests that Duncan will not see the sun again (since he will be dead).

Your face . . . strange matters Your looks reveal to others the peculiar
thoughts you are thinking.

beguile the time i.e. deceive everybody.

the serpent Since the serpent is equated with Satan, so, by implication,
is Macbeth.

provided for A deadly pun, meaning taken care of in the sense of
treated with great hospitality then murdered.

my dispatch My management.

nights and days to come/Solely sovereign sway and masterdom The
mention of nights and days is ironic, since later she cannot sleep when
she thinks of the deed. Lady Macbeth and her husband never achieve
the 'sovereign sway' for themselves alone which she asserts here.

To alter favour ever is to fear i.e. changes in your expression may
reveal your cowardice.

Act I Scene 6

Duncan and Banquo arrive at the castle, and are gushingly
welcomed by Lady Macbeth, who is particularly anxious to
impress Duncan with the honour he is doing them and how
much they honour him in return.

Commentary

The scene is effective dramatically because it offers a contrast
with those which preceded it, and with those to come. The
lovingly observant descriptions of the peacefulness and the
'temple-haunting martlet' are of nature at rest; what is to come is
unnatural and restless. Duncan is gracious, Lady Macbeth hypo-
critically obsequious. The words 'honour'd hostess' and the
repetition of this and of the word 'love' may be contrasted with
Lady Macbeth's ominous use of the word 'double'; her coming
abuse of the natural laws of hospitalitiy is given more point by
the fact that it is Lady Macbeth who leads Duncan to Macbeth.
This is the last time we see Duncan in the play.

Hautboys Oboes.

seat Situation.

gentle sense Appreciation.

temple-haunting martlet . . . approve . . . loved mansionry The
house-martin . . . prove . . . loving to build its nest here.

jutty A part that juts out.

coign of vantage Convenient position.

pendent bed, and proceant cradle Images of rest and procreation,
both important in the play, but used lyrically here.

The love that follows . . . we thank as love Though love sometimes
causes us trouble . . . we thank it for being love.

'ild us Reward us.

done . . . done double Key words, the first of action: 'done double'
would in Shakespeare's time, mean 'done strongly' (cf. 'single'
following).

single i.e. weak.

the late dignities i.e. making Macbeth Thane of Cawdor.

hermits i.e. we pray for you, again evidence of Lady Macbeth's
hypocrisy.

coursèd Chased.

purveyor Forerunner.

holp Helped.

in compt/To make their audit These are cold words beside Duncan's
and her own first effusive greeting. The metaphor is of a steward
presenting his account.

Act I Scene 7

Macbeth, thinking about killing Duncan, fears the consequences
and decides not to go ahead with it. He tells Lady Macbeth of his
decision and she chastises him with 'the valour' of her tongue,
accusing him of cowardice. Her determination and the unscrupulous violence of her language, however, makes him
reverse his decision, as she tells him of her plan to get Duncan's
chamberlains drunk so that they, Macbeth and Lady Macbeth,
can murder Duncan.

Commentary

This scene shows the strength of Lady Macbeth's character, and
the uncertainties of Macbeth. His soliloquy, where the breathless
verse rhythms reflect the inner arguments he is using, show him
turning his back on the deed because he fears retribution for the
deed while he lives (he'll risk his immortal soul): because he is
Duncan's kinsman (cousin), subject and host; because Duncan
has been a worthy king; because he is only driven on himself by
ambition. Further, he tells Lady Macbeth that Duncan has
honoured him and that he is now well thought of by everybody.
In a series of taunting questions Lady Macbeth demonstrates
her power over him by subjugating him completely. The assertion, that she would murder her own child if she had committed
herself to Duncan's murder as Macbeth has done, is particularly
horrible, and shows her strength of purpose. The plan reflects
her practical ability, so that Macbeth is moved to admiration.

There is a certain irony in this scene – the great general is a poor leader compared with his wife.

Sewer An officer whose original duty was to taste any dish placed on a royal table.

If it were done . . . The sooner the murder is done and over with the better; but note the rhythm and repetition which conveys the erratic working of Macbeth's thoughts in this state of tension.

trammel up Entangle in a net (there would be no consequences then).

surcease The death (of Duncan), a euphemism, from the legal term meaning 'a cessation of proceedings'.

success Just what it says, the successful murder, but note its ironic likeness in sound to the previous word.

this bank and shoal of time Probably means that life is merely a period in the great eternity of time.

jump the life to come i.e. risk what happens (to the soul) after death.

judgment Punishment, sentence.

To plague th' inventor Torment the person who practised them, carried them out.

Bloody instructions Crimes.

even-handed Balanced, neutral.

Commends . . . poisoned chalice Offers our own evil back to us (metaphor of a sacred chalice containing poison).

double trust Though Macbeth defines this himself, the use of the word 'double' in the play suggests deception as well as strength. (See note p.17).

the deed i.e. Duncan's murder.

faculties Royal powers.

clear Guiltless.

trumpet-tongued i.e. proclaiming (the murder) loudly, like trumpets.

taking-off A euphemism for 'murder'.

Pity Effective personification, and meant to contrast with Lady Macbeth's violent (imagined) murder of a baby in this same scene.

blast Storm.

heavens Cherubins, hors'd/Upon the sightless couriers of the air The metaphor is of cherubim (winged children representing an order of angels) riding on the winds – the 'sightless couriers'.

I have no spur . . . falls on th' other The aerial 'horse' image (see previous note) is succeeded by an earthly one, that of a rider leaping on to the horse's back but in fact overleaping and falling over on the other side – a metaphor for 'ambition'.

worn now in their newest gloss . . . The 'golden opinions' are compared to new clothes which can be flatteringly worn; another in the sequence of clothes images.

Was the hope drunk? . . . green and pale The effect of the taunt is to compare Macbeth's first 'hope' for the crown (already present when the witches' prophecy is uttered) as having become a hangover;

'dress'd' sarcastically takes up Macbeth's clothing image.

account Value.

the ornament of life The crown of Scotland.

Letting 'I dare not . . . The poor cat i' th' adage Letting your fear control what you want, just as the cat (in the proverb) wanted the fish but would not get her feet wet.

I dare do all . . . none I dare do everything that is manly; who dares do more is going beyond human limits.

What beast was't . . . Lady Macbeth implies that Macbeth was below a 'man', that is, he was a beast.

this enterprise to me? i.e. (reveal) the idea of murder to me? She may be referring back to the letter; it is more likely that they have spoken 'further'.

And . . . more the man i.e. if you became king you would be so much more than merely the 'man'.

Did then adhere i.e. provided the opportunity.

their fitness now/Does unmake you The present opportunity for the murder has made you incapable of acting.

to this The murder of Duncan.

screw your courage to the sticking-place This strong image comes from the cross bow; the screwing-up or tightening of the string for action.

wassail so convince Drink and feasting to overcome (them).

the warder of the brain . . . (Memory), which guards the brain, will be converted by drink into fumes in a receptacle – in other words, the chamberlains will not remember what has occurred.

drenched Drowned (in drink).

spongy Drunken.

quell Murder.

undaunted mettle Courageous spirit.

compose Bear.

receiv'd Taken as true.

bend up . . . each corporal agent Strain every nerve (again with an echo of the cross-bow image above).

mock the time with fairest show Delude everybody by appearing happy and innocent. Macbeth is so under his wife's spell that he uses her previous advice to him ('Look like th' innocent flower . . .').

Revision questions

1 In what ways does Scene 1 provide an effective opening to *Macbeth*?

2 Examine closely *four* or *five* examples of figurative language in this act, saying clearly and in detail what they contribute to our appreciation of the play.

3 Describe the different reactions of Macbeth and Banquo to the prophecies of the witches. What do these reactions tell you about each of their characters?

4 Describe in detail Lady Macbeth's reactions to her husband's letter.

5 Compare and contrast the characters of Macbeth and Lady Macbeth up to the end of Act I.

6 Analyse in some depth one of the important soliloquies in this act.

7 Show how Shakespeare creates an atmosphere of tension and evil in any *two* of the scenes in Act I.

Act II Scene 1

Banquo, restless and anxious, fears sleep; he meets Macbeth, and gives him a diamond sent as a special present by Duncan to Lady Macbeth. He reveals that on the previous night he had dreamt of the witches; Macbeth says he doesn't think of them, though he'd like to talk to Banquo about them later. After Banquo leaves, Macbeth has a vision of a dagger and of the forthcoming murder; he hears the bell, the signal for action, and goes to do the deed.

Commentary

The tense atmosphere is conveyed by the darkness, the inward fears of Banquo and by his premonition of evil; his attitude is an open one – he speaks what he feels – whereas Macbeth, who, we know, has pondered on the witches' prophecies, lies. He hints that there will be honour for Banquo if he supports Macbeth in the future, but Banquo, the man of integrity, will only accept honour 'So I lose none'. Macbeth's own feverish anxiety is conveyed by the hallucination of the dagger – the symbol of temptation to murder – and the rhythm of the lines captures the fear he feels in his monstrous commitment to the deed. This soliloquy has powerful visual effects – 'gouts of blood' – and shows Macbeth's own imaginative association with the supernatural and with evil. It contains self-knowledge, analysis, guilty conscience and a terrifying self-accusation, with the guilt surfacing in the next scene after the murder has been committed. Once more we note the fundamental contrast between Macbeth and Banquo, between deception and violence on the one hand, loyalty and honour on the other. *Honour* is the index to Banquo's character, and one of the key words in the play.

take't Believe that.

husbandry . . . candles Economy . . . stars (it is a dark night, suitable for the dark deed).

Take thee that too i.e. Banquo hands Fleance his shield or his dagger.

summons Command (to sleep).

merciful Powers Good angels (to combat the evil of the devil's agents, the witches).

cursed thoughts . . . repose Evil dreams . . . during sleep.

unusual pleasure Remarkably generous.

largess to your offices 'Tips' to your servants' quarters.

hostess Note again the ironic use of the word, and the fact that Duncan's last act is a gift to the treacherous instigator of his murder.

shut up . . . content Finished (that day, feeling happy and secure).

Being unprepared . . . have wrought As we weren't prepared, our desire to provide fitting hospitality for Duncan was not fulfilled.

entreat an hour to serve i.e. find the time to discuss.

cleave to my consent when 'tis i.e. support my views (when we discuss the matter).

My bosom franchis'd and allegiance clear My heart free (from evil) and my loyalty to the King unstained.

counsell'd Advised.

Is this a dagger . . . ? Note the question – Macbeth is *fearful* of what he thinks he sees.

fatal . . . sensible to feeling as to sight? Terrifying . . . capable of being felt (touched) as well as being seen?

heat-oppressed Feverish.

marshall'st me the way that I was going i.e. (the dagger) directs him towards the door of Duncan's room.

Mine eyes are made the fools o' th' other senses/Or else worth all the rest If my eyes see a dagger which does not exist, then my other senses, for example, touch, mock them; but the vision of the dagger may be more significant, and demonstrate more than the senses can (it may be 'showing' him what he has to do).

dudgeon . . . gouts Handle . . . drops.

the bloody business which informs i.e. the prospect of the murder causes this shape (the dagger) to appear.

half-world i.e. this hemisphere.

curtained Curtain surrounded beds in Shakespeare's time but the image is of peace, and anticipates Duncan in bed asleep before the murder.

Witchcraft . . . Pale Hecate's offerings Witches . . . make their sacrificial rites to their goddess Hecate, who is also goddess of the moon and thus 'pale' in the light.

Tarquin's ravishing strides . . . Tarquin, last of the legendary Kings of Rome, whose rape of Lucrece caused his people, the Tarquins, to be expelled from Rome. Shakespeare wrote a long poem on the subject, *The Rape of Lucrece* (1594).

prate of my where-about i.e. tell of my doings, reveal where I am.
take the present horror . . . Be appropriate to the present horror.
Words to the heat of deeds too cold breath gives i.e. the longer we
  spend talking about something the less inclined we are to act.

Act II Scene 2

Lady Macbeth is awaiting her husband's return after the murder
of Duncan; when he enters we see that his nerves are shattered
by the enormity of what he has done. Moreover he has brought
the daggers with him. Hysteria and guilt have made him incapable of further action, though Lady Macbeth urges him to wash
his hands and replace the daggers beside the grooms. He is
demoralized, and Lady Macbeth herself takes the daggers,
saying that she will smear the grooms with blood. A knocking is
heard at the gate, Lady Macbeth returns, acts promptly, and gets
Macbeth off to change into his dressing-gown.

Commentary

Lady Macbeth is completely in command of herself (and subsequently of Macbeth). Tension is high throughout this scene, the
broken lines of verse spoken by Lady Macbeth conveying her
snatched thoughts and reactions, the noises, the 'voice' and
finally the knocking bringing home to them both the reality –
the fact that the murder will shortly be discovered. Lady Macbeth is practical and brave, covering Macbeth's failure to keep
exactly to their plan, but putting things right herself; Macbeth
broods deeply, his offence against God and man sticking in his
mind, the blood confirming his permanent guilt. The scene is
full of dramatic irony, with Lady Macbeth referring to madness
and to water cleansing them both; she is to become mad (Act V
Scene 1) when nothing can cleanse her mind. Macbeth's poetic
invocation to sleep – representing a peace he will never know
again; his hearing a voice (an aural equivalent to the vision of the
dagger); his fearing the hands that will pluck out his eyes – all
are conveyed with dramatic immediacy. If we admire and condemn Lady Macbeth, we yet feel some compassion for the murderer himself.

quenched Put out their fires (in drink).
the fatal bellman The owl, bird of ill-omen, is here compared to the
  bellman who visited condemned prisoners on the night before their
  death.

surfeited i.e. drunk.

mock their charge Betray their responsibility (of guarding the King).

possets Night drink made from a mixture of ale, milk, eggs, sugar.

Death and Nature do contend i.e. it is doubtful whether they are just sleeping heavily or are dead.

Confounds i.e. ruins.

Had he not resembled . . . I had done't A note of humanity in Lady Macbeth – Duncan's likeness to her own father makes her hold back from the actual murder herself.

a sorry sight/A foolish thought Lady Macbeth tries lightly, through quick word-play here, to turn Macbeth's thoughts from the misery occasioned by his deed.

address'd them Got ready again (to go to bed).

these hangman's hands In Shakespeare's time the hangman had to draw and quarter his victims, and would therefore have his hands covered in blood.

List'ning i.e. hearing (them).

After these ways: so, it will make us mad. If we think like this, we'll become mad – an ironic comment in view of what happens to Lady Macbeth and Macbeth's own increasingly 'mad' actions.

ravell'd sleave Tangled skein.

The death of each day's life . . . Note the metaphors of the next few lines which cover refreshment of the body and the mind both in terms of healing and food. It is the poetry of anguish.

Shall sleep no more, Macbeth shall sleep no more! This 'prophecy' ironically also comes true – Macbeth has terrible dreams, and Lady Macbeth's 'sleep' reveals her guilt and her broken mind (Act V Scene 1).

unbend i.e. diminish, lessen.

brainsickly Ironic, in view of Lady Macbeth's own later 'brain sickness'.

get some water . . . filthy witness Note the phrase, which is to recur in her madness. The 'witness' is the blood.

a painted devil i.e. a picture, drawing of a devil. Lady Macbeth is reprimanding her husband's cowardice.

gild . . . guilt A pun at this moment of crisis. 'Gild' is to cover with a thin layer of gold; later Macbeth refers to Duncan's 'silver skin laced with his golden blood'.

What hands are here? This is the climax of his hysteria – an hallucination of even greater emotional power than that of the dagger.

Neptune's i.e. belonging to the Roman god of the sea.

The multitudinous seas incarnadine i.e. turn all the seas red. A hyperbole that reflects his deep guilt.

the green one red The sea stained red with blood, continuing the hyperbole above.

A little water . . . Ironic, in view of her 'Out, damned spot!' in Act V, Scene 1.

constancy i.e. strength of will.

left you unattended Forsaken you.
night-gown Dressing-gown.
poorly Miserably, without spirit.
To know my deed . . . i.e. I cannot know myself without knowing too
what I have done (therefore I'd rather be 'lost' in my own thoughts).

Act II Scene 3

The knocking continues, and the Porter, obviously suffering
from a hangover, is roused and talks to himself; eventually he
admits Macduff and Lennox, garrulously engaging them in
conversation. When Macbeth appears, Macduff tells him that he
had arranged to call 'timely' on the King, while Lennox reports
the strange, seemingly supernatural happenings of the night.
Macduff returns exclaiming at the horror of Duncan's murder;
the alarm bell is rung, Lady Macbeth and Banquo hear the news
from Macduff, and Macbeth reappears suddenly. He announces
that in his violent anger he has killed the king's attendants – he
calls them the 'murderers' – and Lady Macbeth faints, or affects
to faint, in reaction to her husband's mistake. Malcolm and
Donalbain, the King's sons, fearing suspicion or even death
themselves, decide to flee in different directions.

Commentary

This scene is packed with dramatic action. Notice that the
porter's speech, in prose, is full of word-play and associations
that are a *commentary* on the main action of the play. He is indeed
porter of Hell-gate, if Macbeth is seen as the Devil; his ramblings
effectively delay the discovery, so that with his lascivious
humour and his stumblings and natural comic effects, a degree
of tension is built up in audience and reader. Our laughter is
conditioned by what we know is imminent – the discovery of
murder. Apart from the dramatic irony, the scene also serves
the practical purpose of giving Macbeth and Lady Macbeth the
time to get ready, to appear at the opportune moment in order
to convey maximum innocence. Macbeth has acted unnaturally,
and the unnatural effects in nature outside correspond to this.
Macduff uses Christian imagery to announce his awful discovery, thus adding to the enormity of the crime, while Macbeth
speaks in elaborate, poetic metaphor ('His silver skin laced with
his golden blood') to cover his guilt. Macduff is blunt, forthright,
when he tells Malcolm and Donalbain 'Your royal father's murdered'. Lady Macbeth's faint may be real, since she has just

learned that her husband has killed the attendants; yet it could be feigned in order to draw attention from him, She may feel that he is in error and has overacted his part. Already there is suspicion. Lennox says that it 'seem'd' as if the attendants had killed Duncan, and Malcolm and Donalbain certainly suspect Macbeth, though their own flight serves to transfer suspicion to them and plays into Macbeth's hands. Banquo makes a strong assertion of his integrity with his indictment of 'treasonous malice'.

old i.e. frequent – the Porter is grumbling about his usual 'old' task of key-turning.

Belzebub Satan.

Here's a farmer that hanged himself . . . the farmer killed himself because, having hoarded his crops in the hope that prices would rise he found that next season crops were plentiful and prices were therefore low.

napkins enow Enough handkerchiefs.

th' other devil's name? In his hung-over state the porter cannot recall the name of another devil apart from Beelzebub.

an equivocator Probably a reference to the Jesuit, Henry Garnet, who, when on trial in March 1606 for his part in the Gunpowder Plot, equivocated, that is, gave evidence which amounted to perjury.

the scales i.e. of Justice.

treason enough . . . equivocate to heaven Another reference to Garnet, who was found guilty of treason and hanged.

stealing out of a French hose Skimping his cloth for making breeches, stealing some of the material he had been given in order to make them narrow after the French fashion of the time.

roast your goose Heat your iron (but there is also a sexual innuendo – catch venereal disease).

the primrose way to th' everlasting bonfire i.e. the flowery path to hell.

remember the Porter i.e. don't forget to tip me.

second cock Three a.m.

nose-painting i.e. you get a red nose if you drink too much.

an equivator with lechery . . . giving him the lie The Porter's bawdy remarks mean that drink provokes sexual desire but removes the capacity to indulge it, finally fulfilling lechery only in sleep (by dreaming), and thus 'overthrowing' the desire.

gave thee the lie Macduff is taking up the last phrase in its wrestling sense of the porter being overcome by drink.

requited Paid back.

he took up my legs sometime i.e. he was lifted by drink, just as a wrestler lifts his opponent, but managed to throw him off or even, more crudely, to overcome drink by 'throwing up'.

timely At an early hour.

slipp'd the hour Arrived late.

The labour we delight in physics pain Our happiness in doing
  something we enjoy makes us accept the hard work involved.

limited Proper.

appoint so Arrange to.

Lamentings heard i' th' air i.e. evidence of the unnatural effects
  produced in nature, which mirror the unnatural events within
  Macbeth's castle.

dire combustion i.e. terrible confusion.

New-hatched to th' woeful time, the obscure bird i.e. the owl,
  portender of death, emerged (to screech all night) to contribute to the
  terrible happenings.

feverous and did shake Metaphor comparing an earthquake to the
  ague of high fever.

My young remembrance . . . My short memory can't recall anything
  like it.

The Lord's anointed Temple . . . A reference to the Bible (Samuel
  24,10, and 2 Corinthians 6,16) and to the Divine Right of Kings,
  peculiarly appropriate this early in the reign of James I (1603–1625).

a new Gorgon The Gorgon turned to stone all who looked on her but
  she was slain by Perseus, who used his shield as a mirror.

this downy sleep, death's counterfeit An unconscious echo by
  Macduff of Macbeth's invocation to sleep in Act II, Scene 2.

The great doom's image . . . walk like sprites Doomsday . . . walk like
  spirits (for this is Doomsday).

countenance Look upon.

parley Discussion.

O gentle lady A fine piece of dramatic irony, since Lady Macbeth
  unknown to Macduff instigated the murder.

What! in our house? Either a slip by Lady Macbeth (who thinks guilt
  will attach to her and her husband because it happened there) or a
  seemingly innocent, spontaneous reaction.

Had I but died an hour before this chance . . . If I had died before this
  happening, I would have been blessed.

mortality Human life. Macbeth is trying to impress by his grief, but the
  words apply to him later, and he unconsciously voices the right words
  too, 'renown' and 'grace'.

toys Trifles.

lees . . . vault Dregs . . . the earth covered by the sky.

badged Marked.

Th' expedition of my violent love/Outrun the pauser, reason The
  haste to snow my love of Duncan (by killing them) overcame my
  rational thoughts, which would have delayed me.

silver skin . . . golden blood See comment after scene summary above.

wasteful i.e. laying waste, destroying.

Steep'd in the colours of their trade Murderers covered in blood.

Unmannerly breeched with gore Improperly covered to the hilts with
  blood.

Help me hence, ho! See comment, after the scene summary above,
  about this real or feigned faint.
that most may claim/This argument for ours? We have the greatest
  right to take part in this discussion?
auger-hole Tiny, unsuspected place.
not yet brew'd i.e. (we have) not yet had time for our sorrow to mature.
Upon the foot of motion Started to make itself known.
our naked frailties . . . Clothed ourselves physically because it is cold,
  and prepared ourselves mentally.
undivulged pretence Unrevealed plan.
manly readiness i.e. armour (in case of further violence).
an unfelt sorrow . . . the false man does easy i.e. Malcolm is already
  expressing his suspicion of treachery and hypocrisy in the 'false man'
  (Macbeth) who can easily feign grief.
There's daggers in men's smiles . . . Donalbain too takes up the theme
  of treachery and relates it to Macbeth – 'the near in blood/The nearer
  bloody'. Remember that Macbeth is Duncan's cousin.
This murderous shaft that's shot . . . The implication is that things
  have only just started, and that they – Malcolm and Donalbain – would
  be wise to get away.
dainty Fussy.
shift away Clear off unnoticed.
warrant in that theft i.e. justification in 'stealing' away.

Act II Scene 4

Ross talks with an old man, who says that he has never seen
anything like the unnatural happenings that accompanied 'the
deed that's done'. Macduff arrives to tell Ross that Malcolm and
Donalbain are suspected of the murder, that Macbeth has
already been named King and gone to be invested but that he,
Macduff, will not be attending the coronation.

Commentary

This brief scene indicates the passage of time between the murder and Macbeth's coming to the throne, with an emphasis again
on the supernatural and unnatural in nature that has mirrored
the unnatural act of murder. It acts as a chorus to the main
action of the play. There is a strong symbolic association with the
crucifixion of Christ, with darkness replacing sunlight. Macduff's refusal to go to Scone indicates his suspicions of Macbeth,
while Ross's time-serving opportunism is certainly underlined by
his saying that he will attend the coronation. Note Macduff's use
of the clothes imagery, in a sarcastic thrust at Ross, to show his

own loyalty to the past. The old man's final blessing is a Christian comment on acts and actions that seem to come from the Devil; we are far away from the court and intrigue, but the prevailing evil is the talk of all.

sore Terrible.

trifled former knowings Made previous events seem trivial.

the heavens, as troubled with man's act . . . bloody stage A punning sequence which shows (a) heaven viewing the unnatural acts of man and (a) the play metaphor being used (act, stage), heavens being the roof of the stage.

the travelling lamp i.e. the sun.

darkness . . . entomb . . . light Reminiscent of the Crucifixion of Christ (see critical commentary after scene summary above).

towering in her pride of place Falconry terms, meaning mounting high in circles to the highest place or 'pitch'.

mousing owl i.e. one which sticks near the ground to prey on mice.

minions i.e. favourites (finely-bred horses).

broke their stalls . . . Contending 'gainst obedience Smashed their stables . . . rebelling against their training.

pretend i.e. intend.

suborn'd Paid (to commit the murder).

which puts upon them Which suggests, implies (but notice that the way Macduff puts it means that he is in doubt).

ravin up Greedily devour.

Thine own life's means Their own succession and the succession of their heirs.

nam'd Chosen.

Scone The famous stone of Scone (an ancient city located about two miles north of the modern Perth) served for many ages as the place where the kings of Scotland were crowned; the stone was removed by Edward I and forms part of the British coronation chair in Westminster Abbey.

Colme-kill The 'cell' of Columba, burial-place of the ancient Kings of Scotland.

Fife Macduff's home. He is indicating that he will not be attending Macbeth's coronation.

our old robes The clothing image which runs through the play, here indicating that his loyalty is to the previous king, and implying that this one's régime may be severe.

benison Blessing.

That would make good or bad . . . Perhaps a sarcastic comment on Ross's time-serving – his acceptance of Macbeth.

Revision questions

1 Indicate the main qualities of character shown both by Macbeth and Lady Macbeth in the course of this act.

2 Do you find the porter's scene funny, dramatically effective or both? Give reasons for your answer and refer closely to the text.

3 What part does the *supernatural* play during Act II?

4 Give an account of Shakespeare's use of *dramatic irony* in Act II.

5 What do we learn of the character of (a) Banquo and (b) Macduff in Act II?

6 Write an essay on either (a) Macbeth's hallucination and hysteria or (b) Lady Macbeth's reactions before and after the murder of Duncan.

7 In what ways does Scene 4 provide an important commentary on what has happened and its results?

Act III Scene 1

In the palace at Forres Banquo ponders on Macbeth's success and reveals his suspicions of him. When Macbeth enters he invites Banquo to a banquet he is giving that evening, and then finds out what he intends to do with his time until the feast, and whether Fleance will be with him or not. Macbeth reveals his own insecurity while Banquo lives – for the prophecy said that Banquo's issue would be kings – and then interviews his hired murderers, whom he has already turned against Banquo, saying that Banquo and Fleance must be killed before the banquet.

Commentary

Banquo's soliloquy at the beginning of the scene sheds some light on his character, for though he suspects Macbeth, he seems to hope that since the prophecies about Macbeth have come true, those concerning him (Banquo) may come true too. His assertion of loyalty to Macbeth is a deliberately ironic echo of Macbeth's previous assertion of loyalty to Duncan, while Macbeth's cunning is shown in two ways: (a) his cross-questioning of Banquo in order to find out his movements and Fleance's, and (b) his reference to Malcolm and Donalbain, which shows him keeping up suspicion against them in his listener's mind.

By inviting Banquo to the feast Macbeth means of course, to allay any suspicion that he has any designs upon Banquo; yet his own decision to spend the time alone is bound in itself to cause suspicion. His bitterness – he has no heirs to succeed him but fears that Banquo's heirs will – is shown in his soliloquy, yet this also contains a rare acknowledgement of Banquo's 'royalty of nature', a recognition that *his integrity* is unshakeable compared with his own. Macbeth's dialogue with the murderers shows how completely unscrupulous he is.

stand in thy posterity Stay in your family.
shine Shed fulfilment.
verities . . . oracles truths . . . prophets.
Sennet A set of notes (strictly seven) on a trumpet.
all-thing Totally.
solemn Ceremonious.
indissoluble tie Loyalty to Macbeth *and* shared knowledge of the witches. Banquo is being deliberately ambiguous.
grave and prosperous i.e. serious and invaluable.
go not my horse the better i.e. if my horse doesn't go fast enough.
twain Two.
bestow'd To be found.
strange invention i.e. saying that Macbeth committed the murder.
cause of State/Craving us jointly State matters which will require both of us to deal with them.
master of his time Employ himself as he wishes.
To make society the sweeter welcome In order to make company all the more pleasant to me (I will keep myself alone).
To be thus is nothing, but to be safely thus i.e. to be King outwardly is no good unless I am completely secure.
royalty of nature An acknowledgement of Banquo's worth, and perhaps an admission of his own lack of true 'royalty'.
Reigns Following on from the above. Since it is Macbeth who reigns, the word is used ironically.
Genius is rebuk'd Guardian spirit is put down.
Mark Antony's was by Caesar The source is Plutarch's *Life of Antony*. In Shakespeare's *Antony and Cleopatra* Antony was finally defeated by Octavius Caesar.
fruitless . . . barren i.e. because he has no child to succeed to the throne.
unlineal Not of my line or family.
fil'd Defiled, become corrupt.
rancours in the vessel Poisoned my own cup.
mine eternal jewel My immortal soul.
the common Enemy of man Satan, the Devil.
come, fate, into the list/And champion me to th' utterance i.e. I challenge fate to fight with me to the death.
under fortune Kept you down.
I made good to you I convinced you of.
pass'd in probation with Spent time proving.

borne in hand Misled.
the instruments People, agents.
half a soul . . . notion Half-witted person . . . mind.
point of i.e. reason for.
let this go? i.e. ignore it?
gospell'd Humbly Christian as to love those who are your enemies, (an echo of Matthew 5,44).
catalogue List.
Shoughs, water-rugs, and demi-wolves are clept Shaggy dogs, shaggy water-dogs, halfbreed wolf-dogs are named.
valu'd file Classified list with values.
housekeeper Watchdog.
clos'd Placed.
Particular addition from the bill Distinguishing name to each one apart from the list.
station in the file Position on the list.
Whose execution takes your enemy off The carrying out of which kills your enemy (Banquo).
Who wear our health . . . were perfect We are undermined while he lives but would be freed from this if he were dead.
tugg'd Pulled about.
set Gamble.
bloody distance Deadly enemy, a use of the fencing term which defines the distance between the antagonists.
my near'st of life My inmost being.
avouch Swear to.
wail his fall Mourn his death.
do make love Woo you (to help me).
The perfect spy o' th' time Precise indication of the exact time.
something from i.e. some distance away from.
always thought . . . clearness Always bearing in mind that I must be freed from suspicion.
rubs nor blotches No unevenness or clumsiness.
absence Death (is just as important to me).
Resolve yourselves apart Prepare yourselves a little way off.

Act III Scene 2

Lady Macbeth tries to raise Macbeth's spirits, nagging him because he has been spending his time alone, telling him not to brood and that 'what's done is done'. He in return tells her to pay particular attention to Banquo at the banquet that night, and agrees with her that Banquo and Fleance are vulnerable. He says that 'a deed of dreadful note' will be carried out shortly.

Commentary

Lady Macbeth herself now seems somewhat insecure, though
her advice to her husband shows that she sees he is weighed
down by conscience. He is, of course, bothered by his terrible
dreams, but though he voices this to his wife he has already
planned the murder of Banquo. Whereas they planned everything together before, he is now acting on his own without
confiding in her. This contributes to the dramatic irony. In his
final mention of the coming deed he reverts to his earlier images
of light, darkness and the invocation to the supernatural in the
form of 'black Hecate'.

From now on Macbeth dominates the action. The lack of
confidence between Macbeth and Lady Macbeth is paralleled by
Lady Macbeth's feeling that once everything is over it should be
forgotten, whereas Macbeth feels that he must go on killing in
order to make himself secure. The further irony is that whereas
Lady Macbeth's conscience leads to madness Macbeth has come
to ride roughshod over his conscience. In effect their earlier
roles in the play are reversed.

content Satisfaction.
by destruction dwell in doubtful joy By destroying (killing) someone,
  gain only happiness filled with apprehension.
sorriest Miserable.
Using Having.
without all remedy Beyond cure.
What's done is done Ironic, since she is later to brood about what they
  have done, but also an echo of Macbeth's 'If it were done, when 'tis
  done' of Act I, Scene 7.
scorch'd Slashed with a knife.
close Become joined once more.
her former tooth The poisonous fangs before she (the snake) was
  slashed.
let the frame of things disjoint The structure of the universe collapse.
both the worlds suffer Earth and heaven collapse.
these terrible dreams i.e. about (his) murdering Duncan.
to gain our peace To achieve our ambition.
the torture of the mind to lie i.e. as if he were on that instrument of
  torture, the rack.
restless ecstasy Tossing to and fro deliriously.
foreign levy An army of foreign mercenaries.
sleek o'er your rugged looks i.e. present a smooth undisturbed
  appearance.
Let your remembrance apply Make sure you single Banquo out.
Present him eminence Distinguish him, honour him.

Unsafe the while that we . . . lave We are so insecure . . . wash.
vizards Masks.
scorpions Stings, tortures.
Nature's copy's not eterne Their hold on life is not permanent.
jocund Joyful (ironically, at the thought of the death of Banquo and
  Fleance).
shard-born Bred on dung *and* lifted by its wing-cases.
dearest chuck A term of endearment, but at the same time he is not
  confiding in her.
seeling The falconer sews up the eyes of the hawk until he is properly
  trained.
Scarf up Cover, as with a blindfold.
bloody and invisible hand i.e. of the falconer. The metaphor
  continues, with the hand *invisible* to the blinded hawk and *bloody* from
  the act of seeling.
Cancel . . . that great bond/Which keeps me pale Legal term, but the
  meaning is 'break the moral law by which Banquo and Fleance live and
  which keeps me in dread'.
the crow The rook.
Night's black agents Forces of evil.
Things had begun . . . What has started in evil can only be
  strengthened by more evil.

Act III Scene 3

In this brief scene Banquo is murdered but Fleance escapes. A
third murderer appears, obviously sent by Macbeth to see that
the other two do their work. The murderers reveal that
Fleance's escape has cost them more than half their reward.

Commentary

There is a curious emphasis in the verse being spoken before the
murder ('The west yet glimmers with some streaks of day'), for
the poetic quality in the mouth of such a villain gives the whole
scene an ironic and ghastly flavour. The putting out of the light
is a simple reflection of the murder of Banquo, of taking life in
darkness, in evil action, which is one of the major themes of the
play.

delivers/Our offices Brings us our instructions.
To the direction just Precisely according to Macbeth's orders.
lated i.e. belated.
timely In good time.
the note of expectation The list of guests who will be there.
Was't not the way? Wasn't it the right thing to do?

Best half of our affair More than half of our reward.

Act III Scene 4

The banquet scene, with Macbeth welcoming his guests, after which he slips aside to a door to speak to the First Murderer. He learns that Banquo has been killed but Fleance has escaped. He returns to the table, is chided by Lady Macbeth for his absence and sees shortly afterwards the ghost of Banquo sitting in his seat. He becomes distracted, but Lady Macbeth reasons with him and explains away this strange aberration to the company. She tells Macbeth that it is his imagination, but his courage deserts him when the ghost appears to him again. After the company has been diplomatically dispersed by Lady Macbeth, Macbeth tells her that Macduff 'denies his person/At our great bidding'. Macbeth has spies everywhere, and intends to seek out the witches again.

Commentary

The dramatic tension of the scene is cleverly maintained and balanced by Lady Macbeth's resourcefulness in explaining Macbeth's distraction, and the violence of Macbeth's visionary experience, an immediate and unexpected revelation of his guilt. Macbeth's hypocrisy is shown by his first reference to Banquo ('the grac'd person'), Lady Macbeth's cleverness by her telling the company that her husband will be worse if anyone speaks to him. Her upbraiding of him is similar to that immediately after the murder, but here his private guilt is being displayed publicly.

The reappearance of the ghost subtly follows Macbeth's second mention of Banquo, the irony being that only Macbeth can see the vision ('What sights, my Lord?' asks Ross, but he is headed off by Lady Macbeth). We see Macbeth consolidating power by his network of spies, but the mention of Macduff may mean that opposition is already gathering head. Lady Macbeth's reference to 'the season of all natures, sleep' poignantly echoes Macbeth's own invocation to sleep in Act II Scene 2.

degrees Positions at table, arranged according to rank.
at first/And last Once for all.
her state (Lady Macbeth will remain in) the chair of state.
require her welcome Request her to welcome (the guests).
Both sides are even Numbers on each side of the table are the same.

large Free.

'Tis better thee without, than he within i.e. it is better that the blood is on your face than still in Banquo.

nonpareil Unequalled.

my fit My worry, anxiety.

perfect Secure.

founded Safe.

As broad and general as the casing air As free and without restraint as the surrounding air.

cabin'd, cribb'd Imprisoned, shut in a hut.

saucy Insolent.

safe? i.e. dead? (note the irony).

trenched Deep cut.

a death to nature Enough to cause a man's death.

grown serpent . . . worm Banquo . . . Fleance.

hear ourselves again Discuss it further.

the feast is sold, That is not often vouch'd . . . welcome The feast that is given without constant assurances of welcome might just as well be bought and paid for.

From thence i.e. when one is away from home.

ceremony i.e. courtesy, politeness.

remembrancer A reference perhaps to the three Remembrancers of the Exchequer. Here Macbeth is thanking his wife for 'reminding' him of his duties.

good digestion wait on appetite Enjoy this feast.

our country's honour roof'd i.e. all the Scots nobles under one roof.

grac'd Gracious.

challenge Criticize.

Thou can'st not say I did it Technically, he didn't kill Banquo, but employed others to.

upon a thought Soon, shortly.

extend his passion Prolong his fit.

O proper stuff! Nonsense, rubbish.

air-drawn dagger Drawn through the air (see Act II Scene 1).

flaws Quick squalls (of unpredictable behaviour).

Authoris'd by her grandam Sanctioned by her grandmother.

If charnel-houses . . . maws of kites If those that we bury return from their burial-places, we shall have to get rid of them by giving them as food to the ravens.

Ere humane statute purged the gentle weal Before human law rid society of evil practice and made it peaceful.

twenty mortal murthers on their crowns Deadly wounds in their heads (also see this scene for Banquo's 'twenty trenched gashes on his head').

push us from our stools A reference to the fact that the ghost occupies the seat – and his descendants will occupy the throne.

lack you i.e. miss your attention.

all . . . all Good wishes to everybody.

Avaunt! Go away!

speculation Sight informed by intelligence.

custom i.e. habit.

arm'd i.e. horned.

th' Hyrcan tiger From Hyrcania, a district by the Caspian Sea.

but that i.e. anything but Banquo's shape.

dare me to the desert . . . challenge me to fight to the death.

if trembling I inhabit then If I am still trembling within (from fear).

The baby of a girl i.e. a child's doll.

displac'd the mirth Broken up the happiness.

admir'd i.e. remarkable.

overcome i.e. come over, cast a shadow over.

strange/Even to the disposition that I owe A stranger even to my own nature – I hardly know myself.

mine is blanch'd i.e. my cheek is pale.

order Rank, degree.

It will have blood The murder of Banquo will lead to bloodshed.

Stones i.e. grave-stones.

trees to speak i.e. reveal the secret (of the murder).

Augures, and understood relations Prophecies and the discovery of things that relate to each other.

magot-pies Magpies.

choughs Crows.

The secret'st man of blood A reference to the concealed, hidden murder being discovered.

at odds with the morning i.e. dawn.

How say'st thou . . . What do you say to/think of . . .

by the way Casually (but since he refers immediately after this to his own spies, presumably Macbeth had direct knowledge).

fee'd i.e. bribed, paid.

betimes Early.

All causes shall give way Everything will be subordinate (to my main purpose).

strange things . . . may be scann'd Macbeth, thinking of the murder of Macduff, wishes to act quickly and not think too much about it; if he did, it might prevent action.

season Seasoning *or* preservation.

self-abuse i.e. self-deception.

the initiate fear that wants hard use i.e. the fear of the beginner who lacks practice which hardens one.

young in deed Only just beginning (an ominous comment on his own capacity for unscrupulous action).

Act III Scene 5

Hecate, the goddess of witchcraft, reprimands the witches for not keeping her informed of their dealings with Macbeth; she then tells them to meet her the next morning, since Macbeth is coming to hear his destiny from them.

Commentary

This brief scene in rhyming couplets is arguably not Shakespeare's. It contributes nothing to the dramatic tension and, because of its simple and uncharacteristic language, is only feebly supportive of the supernatural atmosphere.

beldams Hags.
close Secret.
A wayward son i.e. Macbeth.
Acheron An appropriate name for a murky pool near Macbeth's castle, since Acheron was the river of the underworld in classical mythology.
dismal and a fatal Disastrous and deadly.
profound Deep, ready to fall.
sleights Artifices, tricks.
security Lack of anxiety to the point of being over confident.

Act III Scene 6

Lennox confides in a lord his suspicions of Macbeth, indicating that these have been roused by Macbeth's own actions. Macduff has gone to England to enlist aid, and Lennox prays that through God and this aid Scotland will be returned to peace.

Commentary

Macbeth's tyranny is demonstrated by the lord's speech, which confirms Macbeth's own boast that he has spies everywhere. Lennox's speech traces Macbeth's crimes, but with a superbly ironic emphasis – both speakers refer to Macbeth as a tyrant – yet the scene is full of hope and the promise of action, with dramatic tension increased as we feel the opposition building up against Macbeth.

have but hit ... farther Agree with your judgements, and you can come to your own conclusions.
strangely borne Carried on in a peculiar manner.
marry Indeed.
Men must not walk too late An ominous comment on the state of Scotland under Macbeth.
want the thought Help believing.

fact i.e. deed.
tear i.e. kill.
thralls Slaves.
borne i.e. carried off.
under his key In his power.
should Would certainly.
broad Frank.
'cause Because.
bestows i.e. hides, is living.
holds the due of birth Withholds his right of succession.
the most pious Edward Edward the Confessor (1002–66).
the malevolence of fortune nothing/Takes from his high respect His
  loss of the throne does not detract from the respect in which he is held.
To ratify the work i.e. with Heaven blessing the action (against
  Macbeth).
free honours Be rewarded justly, not for servile actions.
and with an absolute . . . turns me his back The frowning messenger
  turns to go back to his master, carrying Macduff's curt answer ('Not I').
that clogs me i.e. that makes me suffer – the messenger fears ill-
  treatment when he gives Macbeth the bad news of Macduff's refusal.
him to a caution, t'hold what distance . . . i.e. make him cautiously
  keep at some distance from Macbeth.

Revision questions

1 What qualities in Macbeth's character are particularly evident
in Act III?
2 What use does Shakespeare make of contrast – in character
and language – in Act III?
3 Write an essay on the actions and reactions of Lady Macbeth
in Scenes 2 and 4, indicating whether or not she is still an
influence on her husband.
4 Write a detailed analysis of one of Macbeth's speeches in this
act, indicating what it tells us of his present and future actions.
5 Compare and contrast Scene 6 with Scene 4 in Act II.
6 In what ways is the banquet scene 'the beginning of the end'
for Macbeth?
7 Do you find anything of dramatic interest in Scene 5? Can it
be successfully related to the rest of the play?

Act IV Scene 1

The witches meet at a house in Forres and circle their cauldron,
concocting the spell for Macbeth; he arrives and demands
answers to his questions. They conjure the first apparition,

which warns Macbeth to beware of Macduff; the second, the bloody child, says that 'none of woman born/Shall harm Macbeth', while the third says that Macbeth will not be defeated until Birnam Wood comes against Dunsinane. Macbeth is in part comforted (he thinks he has what Hecate called 'security'), but at his request a 'show' reveals the heirs of Banquo, eight kings. After they disappear, Lennox brings word that Macduff has fled to England. Macbeth immediately determines to attack his castle and put his wife and children to death.

Commentary

The supernatural atmosphere, the incantation of the witches, make this a gruesome and terrifying scene even before Macbeth enters. Now dependent on the witches Macbeth demands prophecies rather than has them (as previously) thrust upon him. The light verse of the incantation gives way to Macbeth's opening words; harsh, abrasive, an invocation to evil. The first prophecy is soon to be fulfilled (Macbeth knows that he has to fear Macduff, and has it confirmed when he hears that he has fled to England); the irony of the second prophecy is to be demonstrated later (Act V, Scene 8) when Macduff reveals that he was 'untimely ripp'd' from his mother's womb, and there is the same irony in the third prophecy (Act V, Scene 5). Macbeth's decision to have Lady Macduff and her family murdered shows the depths of degradation to which he has sunk.

brinded Streaked.
hedge-pig Hedgehog.
Harpier Probably from 'Harpy', demonic companion of the third witch.
Swelter'd Sweated out (in its sleep).
Fillet A slice.
fenny Belonging to the fens.
fork Short for 'forked tongue'.
blind-worm's Slow-worm's.
howlet's Baby owl's.
Witches' mummy Parts of bodies of dead witches, mummified.
maw and gulf . . . ravin'd Throat and stomach . . . filled with the prey it has devoured.
slips of yew The seedlings of the yew (believed to be poisonous).
Sliver'd Cut off.
drab i.e. prostitute.
slab Slimy.
chaudron Entrails.

ingredience Ingredients.

pricking of my thumbs Superstition that something is about to happen if you feel some pain in part of the body.

black, and midnight hags i.e. witches practise the black arts, are worshippers of the devil.

untie the winds It was thought that the winds were controlled by witches.

Against the churches i.e. the winds would batter the churches, just as the Devil would batter Christianity.

yesty Foamy.

Confound Ruin.

navigation Ships.

lodg'd Laid flat.

slope Bend.

germens Seeds.

till destruction sicken Until destruction is surfeited with itself.

farrow Litter.

sweaten Sweated.

an armed head Prophetic indeed – Macbeth's, which is to be cut off by Macduff.

caution i.e. warning.

harp'd Guessed.

a bloody child Macduff, 'untimely ripp'd' from his mother's womb.

I'll make assurance double sure/And take a bond of fate i.e. to make himself secure by heeding the warning of the First Apparition and having Macduff killed, thus binding Fate to its promise.

a child crowned, with a tree in his hand Malcolm ('Let every soldier hew him down a bow' (Act V, Scene 4).

the round and top The crown.

Birnam Ten miles (17km) or so north-east of Perth, and Dunsinane hill is some six miles (10km) north of Perth, the two being some ten miles (17km) apart.

impress i.e. press into service.

bodements Prophecies.

Rebellious dead Probably a reference to the dead Banquo, whose ghost appeared at the banquet.

the lease of Nature Legal metaphor, here meaning 'live out his life normally until it is time to die.'.

eight Kings . . . following i.e. the Stuart line of Kings of Scotland.

Start, eyes! i.e. leap from your sockets.

th' crack o' doom The peal of doomsday.

glass A magic mirror.

two-fold balls and treble sceptres Probably a compliment to James I, alluding to his coronations, first as King of Scotland; then at Westminster. He was the first King of England, Scotland and Ireland, hence the 'treble sceptres'.

blood-bolter'd Hair clotted, matted with blood.

amazedly i.e. in wonder.
sprites Spirits.
antic round Weird dance.
aye For ever.
And damned all those that trust them Dramatic irony, since Macbeth
 himself trusts them.
anticipat'st Forestall.
The flighty purpose never is o'ertook . . . Sudden motives for action
 disappear (unless we act immediately upon them).
firstlings . . . firstlings First idea . . . first actions.
To crown my thoughts with acts . . . To put my ideas into action.
trace him in his line Follow him, his descendants. Macbeth is obsessed
 at being displaced by 'succession', following the show of the eight
 kings.

Act IV Scene 2

Macduff's castle, where Ross has just told Lady Macduff that her
husband has fled. She is worried, bewildered, angry at her
husband's action. When Ross leaves, Lady Macduff talks to her
son, and a messenger enters to warn her of the danger she is in.
The murderers appear, kill the son, and pursue Lady Macduff.

Commentary

This is a finely pathetic scene, for here we have a murder of the
innocents (a reflection of Macbeth's speed of action and his
unscrupulous tyranny). Ross shows that he has a heart (he
almost weeps at Lady Macduff's plight), but as usual he serves
his own interests by leaving. The theme of unnatural action is
shown by the murder and by Lady Macduff's bitter words about
Macduff, who hasn't stayed to defend his 'nest' – 'All is the fear,
and nothing is the love.' Dialogue between mother and son is
moving because of the son's precocious reasoning and there is
an incipient hysteria in Lady Macduff's replies, almost as if she
senses that they are living on borrowed time. It is ironic, too, that
although the son's reasoning is sharp, this play deals with ambition, passion and brutality rather than reason.

  Notice that Macbeth has one again directed the murder rather
than commiting it himself, and also the cunning play on the
word 'traitor'; the real 'traitor', Macbeth, is off-stage. Lady Macduff wrily acknowledges that her husband is a 'traitor' to his
family, but when the son denies that his father is a 'traitor' he is
stabbed to death. The play on the word underlines the

unnatural actions, these murders being the most unnatural of all.

when our actions do not . . . Even when we have done nothing.
his titles His possessions.
The natural touch Feelings of natural affection.
the poor wren The bird references in this scene add to the pathos.
All is the fear, and nothing is the love This sums up her bitterness at her husband's desertion.
coz Cousin, relation.
school yourself Show good sense.
The fits o' th' season i.e. how things are at this time.
when we are traitors/And do not know ourselves i.e. when we are traitors and do not recognize the fact.
hold rumour/From what we fear Accept rumour as the expression of what we fear.
Things at the worst . . . Events will stop at a certain point.
My pretty cousin i.e. addressing the son.
It would be my disgrace I should let myself down by weeping.
net, nor lime,/The pit-fall, nor the gin All traps or snares – ironically, she and her son are caught in one now.
Poor birds they are not set for Evidence of the son's precocity – he knows that only birds worth catching for food or for value, are trapped. Part of the irony.
with all thy wit . . . with wit enough for thee With your sense (which is limited) . . . yet good sense for your age.
monkey A term of affection.
Though in your state of honour I am perfect/I doubt Though with your rank I am fully aware/I believe.
To do worse to you were fell cruelty . . . To do you any harm would be monstrous (but evil people are after you).
I am in this earthly world . . . I live here (in Macbeth's Scotland).
unsanctified Another of the Christian echoes which act as a commentary on Macbeth's devilish actions.
shag-hair'd Rough-haired.
egg . . . fry The metaphor of 'egg' (youngster), suggests 'fry' (fish-spawn).

Act IV Scene 3

The longest scene in the play takes us to Macduff, with Malcolm in England. Malcolm questions Macduff about his reasons for leaving his family (he suspects that he may be an agent of Macbeth's) and then says that Scotland would be in a worse state if he (Malcolm) were king. He outlines his vices before giving a picture of the 'king-becoming graces' which a monarch should have. All this is a testing of Macduff, who responds by praising Duncan and his wife (Malcolm's mother) and telling Malcolm that he (Malcolm) is unfit to rule. Malcolm then reveals that he was testing Macduff's loyalty to true principles, and tells him that he has already got English support against Macbeth.

Ross arrives with the news of the murder of Macduff's wife and children – though he takes some time to tell it – and Macduff's grief is made the more poignant by his feelings of guilt at leaving his family unprotected. This adds to his bitterness, and he vows to avenge them by meeting Macbeth face to face.

Commentary

This scene is dramatic and moving, since before Ross's arrival the audience knows what Macduff and Malcolm do not know – that Macduff's family are dead. Malcolm has to be sure of Macduff, hence the testing on a personal and patriotic level. Their long exchange, with its revelations of character, is an admirable non-action prelude to the dramatic entrance of Ross with his terrible news. His delay, whether from sensitivity or fear, raises tension, and the poignant word-play on 'well' and 'peace' enhances the pathos of the disclosure. 'He has no children' followed by 'All my pretty ones?' exactly trace the bewildered, piteous and revengeful reactions of Macduff. Thus the scene moves from discussion to tension to imminent action, a dramatic preparation for the battle scenes to come in the confrontations of the final act. There is also a subtle contrast between the tyrant king and the good king – Edward the Confessor.

mortal Deadly.
Bestride our downfall birthdom Take up arms for the country of our birth.
Strike heaven Assault goodness.
Like syllable of dolour The same cries of grief.
to friend To take my part.
sole Mere.
He hath not touched you yet Dramatic irony – Macbeth has in fact already had Macduff's family murdered.
You may deserve of him through me i.e. he (Macbeth) may reward you for betraying me.
imperial charge Royal commission.
cannot transpose i.e. cannot alter.

Angels are bright still . . . the brightest There are good angels . . . Lucifer.

I have lost my hopes I have given up (if you doubt me).

rawness Unprotected state.

precious motives Deeply valued.

jealousies Doubts.

lay thou thy basis sure Establish yourself completely.

Thy title is affeer'd Your claim is confined.

to boot As well.

gracious England i.e. Edward the Confessor.

more sundry ways than ever In different, more terrible, manner.

grafted . . . open'd Engrafted . . . put forth like buds.

confineless Wide-ranging.

to top Worse than.

Luxurious i.e. lustful.

no bottom No end to, no satisfying.

cistern of my lust My sexual needs.

continent impediments would o'erbear (My lust) would overcome all restraining checks.

Convey Indulge.

the time you may so hoodwink i.e. you may be able to mislead everybody.

to greatness dedicate themselves . . . i.e. make themselves available for your lust (sarcastically said by Macduff).

Ill-composed affection Evilly-made disposition.

staunchless Unquenchable.

his jewels i.e. one man's valuables.

a sauce Stimulus.

forge quarrels Make up arguments.

summer-seeming i.e. in youth, young manhood.

The sword . . . The reason for taking up arms.

foisons Plenty.

your mere own Your royal property.

portable Endurable.

weigh'd Balanced against.

Lowliness Humility.

relish Trace.

division Variation, different appearance.

Pour the sweet milk of concord i.e. destroy agreement, happiness, create havoc.

Uproar Throw into confusion.

untitled tyrant bloody-scepter'd i.e. the usurping King stained with blood.

truest issue Malcolm.

interdiction Acknowledged incapability.

Died every day she liv'd Gave herself up, sacrificed herself to prayer, every day.

passion Grief.
Wip'd the black scruples Removed my evil suspicions.
trains Artifices, lures.
modest wisdom . . . haste My caution holds me back from naive action.
Unspeak mine own detraction Take back my own condemnation of myself.
strangers Unknown.
at a point Prepared for any emergency.
chance of goodness . . . warranted quarrel The chance of winning . . . the justice of our cause.
stay Wait for.
convinces/The great assay of art Defeats the skill of the doctors.
presently amend Immediately recover.
the Evil Scrofula, swollen glands in the neck being the main mark of this killing disease. Edward the Confessor was the first of the Kings of England to try cures by 'touching'; this remained royal practice until 1712.
solicits Entreats.
strangely-visited i.e. having strange diseases.
mere i.e. complete.
a golden stamp i.e. a gold coin.
'tis spoken/To the succeeding royalty he leaves It's said that his successors will inherit (his powers of curing).
a heavenly gift of prophecy A deliberate contrast with the 'unheavenly' prophecies of the witches.
betimes In good time.
But who knows nothing Only those who are ignorant (can afford to smile).
Are made, not mark'd Are uttered unnoticed.
A modern ecstasy An ordinary emotion.
Is there scarce asked for Is hardly ever requested (because death is so common).
flowers in their caps Sprigs of heather in the highlanders' bonnets.
relation/Too nice Too elaborate an account.
an hour's age doth hiss the speaker i.e. news an hour old is stale, therefore the bringer of it is 'hissed', ridiculed.
teems Breeds.
well . . . well at peace Notice the superb irony of well – both euphemisms for 'death'.
niggard Mean.
transport the tidings i.e. bring the news (the murder of Macduff's family) but as usual Ross wraps it up.
were out Ready to fight, rebelling.
Your eye i.e. Your presence.
To doff Shed (another clothing reference).
Gracious England See note p.53.
gives out Proclaims.

would Should, ought to be.
latch Catch.
a fee-grief i.e. grief belonging to one person alone.
quarry The corpses of the game shot in hunting, here the Macduff
  family.
pull your hat upon your brows i.e. the action of pulling his hat over his
  forehead to hide his immediate grief.
Whispers the o'er-fraught heart (Silence) shows a heart too full of
  emotion.
Let's make us med'cines . . . deadly grief Let us cure our grief by
  concentrating on revenge.
He has no children A direct reference to Macbeth; Macduff cannot be
  revenged on him in this way since he has no family to kill.
Hell-kite . . . one fell swoop? Bird of prey killing chickens and their
  dam (mother).
Dispute Fight against.
Naught Worthless.
the whetstone of your sword i.e. let it sharpen your appetite for battle.
Convert Change.
play the woman with mine eyes Weep.
intermission Interval (before I meet Macbeth).
This tune goes manly i.e. this is the right, brave note.
Our lack is nothing but our leave All we have to do is to take our leave
  of the King.
ripe for shaking i.e. for bringing down, like the ripe fruit from a tree.
the Powers above/Put on their instruments The good angels (on our
  side against evil) put on their weapons.

Revision questions

1 Indicate clearly the effect of the witches' prophecies on Macbeth, and look ahead to the next act to see in what ways they are
fulfilled.
2 What are our reactions to Scene 2? Set down your views
clearly and quote from the text to support them.
3 Write a character sketch of Malcolm. Do you think he is
justified in 'testing' Macduff?
4 Say whether you feel pity or anger for Macduff – or both.
Refer closely to the text in your answer.
5 Examine the role of Ross in Scenes 2 and 3. Do you find his
actions justified or not?
6 Write an essay on either (a) the verse of the witches or (b)
dramatic irony or (c) pathos in any scene or scenes in this act.

Act V Scene 1

A doctor in attendance on Lady Macbeth sees her walk in her
sleep and hears her utter her guilty secrets; she returns in her
mind to the past actions of her husband and herself (particularly
the account of and the reaction to the murder in Act II Scene 2).

Commentary

This scene reveals Shakespeare's deep psychological insight into
the subconscious – three hundred years before the theories of
Sigmund Freud became known. Lady Macbeth, hitherto strong
for action and fearless in implementing it, has now suffered a
breakdown. She reveals, by the washing of her hands (to remove
the blood), her mention of Lady Macduff and the knocking, the
secret fears that have been repressed, imprisoned in the
unconscious mind, and which are now released through the
sleep-walking and dreams. Note *all* the references she makes to
the past, and note also that for her, by his continuing career of
unlicensed butchery, Macbeth has 'murdered Sleep'. She had
obviously been kept in ignorance of her husband's actions, but
has found out what he has done, and has become mentally and
emotionally unbalanced as a result. The prose of her anguish is a
suitable medium for its expression, since the strong and determined woman that she was spoke the full-blooded poetry of
action, courage, and ambition for her husband; the broken
woman she now is speaks in the disconnected fragments of prose
that constitute her memory and the frailty of her waning life.

into the field i.e. the battlefield, a reference to Macbeth's troops.
write upon't This could be a letter to Macbeth, or a confession.
perturbation in nature i.e. mental disorder.
the effects of watching The actions of waking.
actual performances The deeds she does.
meet Suitable.
having no witness to confirm my speech Bearing in mind her position
  in Macbeth's household, the gentlewoman is being properly cautious
  about committing herself.
her very guise The way she has behaved before.
light An indication of her fear of darkness.
their sense are shut i.e. she can see nothing.
A spot Of blood. She is thinking back to 'A little water clears us of this
  deed' of Act II, Scene 2.
satisfy my remembrance Provide proof of what I hear.
One; two The clock striking.

afeard Frightened.
none can call our power to accompt i.e. we are too strong to be
  criticized.
the old man i.e. Duncan (we remember that he resembled her father).
mark Observe.
The Thane of Fife had a wife The fact that it is in the past tense shows
  that she more than suspects what has happened to Lady Macduff.
starting Jumpy reaction.
sorely charged Heavily burdened.
dignity value.
practice Ability to cure.
What's done cannot be undone A key phrase, echoing (though
  ironically) 'what's done is done' of Act III, Scene 2.
whisp'rings Rumours.
the divine i.e. a priest (for confession).
annoyance Harm (an obvious anticipation of her suicide).
keep eyes Watch.
has mated i.e. is confused.

Act V Scene 2

A brief scene which shows the Scots' lords armed against Macbeth in the knowledge that Malcolm, Macduff and the English
are coming. They will meet them at Birnam Wood; Macbeth is
known to be fortifying Dunsinane Castle, though his men serve
him not for love or loyalty but because they have to do so.

Commentary

This scene contributes to the tension, the hurry and bustle of
impending battle being the keynote. The mention of Birnam
Wood and Dunsinane is a swift, specific reminder of the witches'
third prophecy (Act IV, Scene 1) and thus increases expectation.
Angus uses the clothes imagery, but here in a distorted sense
which acts as a comparison with Macbeth's own distorted
activity.

dear causes Grounds of action close to their hearts.
bleeding and the grim alarm Battle.
Excite the mortified man Cause the dead to rise again.
file List.
unrough Without beards.
Protest their first Proclaim their manly actions.
lesser hate him Hate him less.
He cannot buckle . . . the belt of rule He cannot control completely
  those under his command.

minutely revolts upbraid his faith-breach Increasingly frequent revolts condemn his own treachery.

like a giant's robe/Upon a dwarfish thief The clothes image brilliantly distorted – Macbeth aspired to be giant (king) but only succeeded in being a thief (by stealing the kingdom from Malcolm).

pestered senses Stricken nerves.

obedience where 'tis truly owed i.e. loyalty to the rightful heir (Malcolm).

the med'cine Malcolm, who will cure the 'sickly weal'.

pour ... purge ... drop Continuing the medicine association, but meaning 'shed our blood to cleanse our country'.

dew the sovereign flower Sustain the royal heir.

Act V Scene 3

Macbeth is determined to brave it out, despite the desertion of many of his soldiers, thinking himself invulnerable because of the third prophecy. He berates the servant when he brings news of the ten thousand English soldiers, calls for Seyton, meanwhile bemoaning his own state and the mere 'mouth-honour' of his own troops. Eventually he asks after Lady Macbeth, and then disdains 'physic' himself as he prepares for the inevitable battle, again reiterating his impregnability 'Till Birnam forest come to Dunsinane'.

Commentary

The scene is steeped in dramatic irony because of Macbeth's reliance on the witches, his violent language demonstrating that latterly he has lived by violence alone. Despite this there is a moment of pure pathos in his 'what-might-have-been' soliloquy as he speaks of 'honour, love, obedience, troops of friends' so that even in our disgust we feel a movement of compassion for the tyrant who should be beyond pity. Even in adversity he still shows his practicality and brutality in having people put to death, but his questioning of the doctor strikes a pathetic note, for his own mind is 'diseased' and the cure he urges for Lady Macbeth applies most terribly to himself. He can never be purged 'to a sound and pristine health' but seeks to throw off his obsessions in the violence of battle.

them fly all All the Thanes flee.

taint Be undermined by.

consequences i.e. circumstances.

epicures i.e. those who live softly, are unused to hardness.

sway by Direct myself by.
loon Worthless fool.
goose look Cowardly appearance.
prick thy face i.e. in order to give it some red blood.
patch Fool.
linen White.
whey-face Pallid.
push Crucial time.
disseat Overthrow.
into the sere Into a withered condition
deep i.e. passionately held, full of hate.
mouth-honour Lip-service.
the poor heart would fain deny The sufferers would like to withhold (from me).
skirr Scour.
thick-coming fancies Frequently occurring hallucinations.
Raze . . . written troubles of the brain Obliterate . . . what is engraved in the mind.
sweet oblivious antidote i.e. a drug bringing about peaceful forgetfulness or oblivion.
Cleanse the stuff'd bosom Rid her clogged heart (of the emotions that fill it).
cast/The water Analyse the urine (to discover what is wrong).
rhubarb, cyme The second is probably 'senna' – both were known to have purgative value.
it The armour.
bane Ruin.

Act V Scene 4

Brief scene of soldiers marching, with Malcolm ordering each to cut down a bough from the wood (Birnam) and 'bear't before him'.

Commentary

Tension, imminent battle is the keynote, with the dramatic and ironic fulfilment of the prophecy brought nearer by Malcolm's instructions to his soldiers.

chambers i.e. within houses or homes.
And bear't before him i.e. as camouflage.
discovery i.e. what is reported.
endure/Our setting down before't Suffer us to lay siege to it.
more and less i.e. everybody, great and small.
constrained things Those who are forced to.

Let our just censures ... true event Our right judgments ... await the
result of the battle (let us not be over-confident).

Thoughts speculative ... strokes must arbitrate Speculations are
based on uncertainties, but actual fighting will decide the issue.

Act V Scene 5

Macbeth waiting in Dunsinane Castle, hears the cry of women,
which announces the fact that Lady Macbeth has taken her own
life. He ponders on the nature of existence – everything leads to
death – and then a messenger enters to tell him that he has seen
Birnam Wood move. Macbeth prepares himself to die bravely.

Commentary

Macbeth's optimism – that his castle can endure a siege – gives
way to his reception of the news that his wife is dead. He swings
now to cynicism as he contemplates the transitory nature of life,
and here again Shakespeare uses the analogy of the stage and
the play in which to embody his ironic comments. We are moved
by the prospect of Macbeth's loneliness and isolation, despite all
his wickedness, but before this can be dwelt on, a dramatic
master stroke indicates the fulfilment of the prophecy – Birnam
Wood has begun to move.

forc'd i.e. reinforced.

dareful Bravely, face to face.

the cry of women The attendants on Lady Macbeth have discovered
that she has killed herself.

have cool'd Have been chilled.

fell of hair i.e. on the skin (the hairs would rise with fear).

dismal treatise A tale of disaster.

Direness Horror.

start me i.e. make me jump.

hereafter Later, not now. A revelation that the hardened Macbeth still
loved his wife.

such a word i.e. such news (that the Queen is dead).

Tomorrow, and tomorrow ... Note how the repetition captures the
monotony of life.

petty pace Small way.

recorded time i.e. the final moment, death.

lighted fools ... dusty death Light shows up foolishness ... to death
(the 'dust to dust' of the burial service).

brief candle i.e. life (and particularly appropriate since Lady
Macbeth's 'light' has been put out).

shadow . . . player . . . upon the stage A stage metaphor, as in *As You Like It*, but here comparing the 'poor player' ('poor' because once he has finished speaking his 'life' on stage is over) and his performance to the brevity of life.

Told by an idiot . . . Signifying nothing This is a cynical view of life but Macbeth *is* moved by his wife's death; she – who was his driving force earlier – has left him and life now 'signifies nothing'.

cling thee Shrivel you up.

sooth True.

I care not if . . . I don't care if (you cause me to suffer the same fate).

I pull in resolution I am no longer confident.

th' equivocation of the fiend The perjury, the misleading ambiguity of the witches.

avouches Asserts.

'gin Begin.

th'estate o'th'world The whole universe.

Act V Scene 6

Malcolm, Macduff and Old Siward on a plain before the Castle, preparing to shed their boughs and fight.

Commentary

This very short scene conveys the activity prior to battle.

show like those you are i.e. reveal yourselves as you are.
harbingers Heralds, forerunners.

Act V Scene 7

Macbeth kills young Siward while Macduff searches for Macbeth. Old Siward brings the news that the Castle has surrendered.

Commentary

Macbeth's bravery is still evident.

Bear-like I must fight the course Bear baiting was a popular Elizabethan sport, the 'course' being the round in which the dogs attack the bear.
wretched Kernes i.e. the poor Irish mercenaries.
staves Lances.
undeeded (The sword) having performed no deed.

bruited Noisily announced.
gently render'd Surrendered without much of a fight.
strike beside us i.e. shot to miss us.

Act V Scene 8

Macbeth encounters Macduff, who reveals that he was 'from his mother's womb/Untimely ripp'd'. Macduff calls upon Macbeth to surrender, but he refuses; they fight, and Macbeth is slain, but not before he has denounced the witches for their 'double sense'. Thus the prophecy has come true.

the Roman fool A reference to the fact that it was considered honourable by the Romans to commit suicide, like Brutus in *Julius Caesar* and Antony in *Antony and Cleopatra*.
lives i.e. living people.
charg'd i.e. burdened.
terms can give thee out i.e. than any words can describe you.
intrenchant Which cannot be cut.
crests Heads.
Untimely ripp'd Prematurely taken (by forceps or Caesarian section) from the mother's body.
cow'd my better part of man i.e. overcome my spirit.
juggling fiends ... palter Cheating devils ... deceive.
Painted upon a pole ... Represented on a cloth.
Hold! From the heralds' 'Ho! Ho!' indicating the end of hostilities.

Act V Scene 9

The final scene of the play, in which Malcolm expresses concern for those who are still missing, and Ross reveals to old Siward that his son has been killed; Old Siward takes pride in his son's wounds. Macduff enters, bearing Macbeth's head; he acclaims Malcolm King of Scotland. Malcolm proclaims the first earls of his realm; promises to uncover all those who helped Macbeth and to recall those who were exiled. He also says that Lady Macbeth is thought to have committed suicide. He finally invites all his nobles to see him crowned at Scone.

Commentary

The play ends on a note of bravery, generosity and with new hope for the future peace of Scotland. Malcolm stands, as we should expect, in contrast to Macbeth; moreover he is a true son of his father Duncan. Note the use of the word 'honour', so often employed ironically in the play; also the image of 'planted' which looks back to Duncan's own imagery and confirms Malcolm's likeness to him.

Notice too the final irony, the crowning-to-be at Scone of the rightful king: Macbeth, we remember, had also been crowned there; but Macduff, who has now helped put all to rights, had denied 'his presence' at the usurper's coronation.

go off Another stage metaphor – exit, die.
cheaply bought i.e. casualties have been light.
unshrinking station i.e. fought in a position and did not shrink from the fight.
on the front i.e. signifying his bravery; if the wounds had been on the back he would have been running away.
hairs A pun on 'heirs' as well.
parted well Died bravely.
the time is free Men are free once again.
thy kingdom's pearl With all your nobles (about you).
Producing forth the cruel ministers Bring out from their hiding places the cruel men (who served Macbeth).
Took off Died, the words before it indicative of suicide.
the grace of Grace The blessing of Goodness, God.
Scone The Stone of Scone, the great Coronation Stone on which the Scottish kings were formerly crowned at Scone. Now housed at Westminster Abbey, under the Chair of St Edward.

Revision questions

1 Trace each reference made by Lady Macbeth to her or her husband's crimes in Scene 1.
2 'That palter with us in a double sense.' How far is Macbeth justified in using these words to describe the witches and their prophecies in the play?
3 How does Shakespeare convey the dramatic tension of battle to reader and audience?
4 Write a careful analysis of the shifts and changes in Macbeth's reactions during this act.
5 Analyse *in detail* one soliloquy uttered by Macbeth in Act V.
6 'This dead butcher, and his fiend-like Queen'. Write an essay saying how far you agree with this estimate of the characters of Macbeth and Lady Macbeth.

General questions

1* What do you find to admire in the character of Lady Macbeth?
*Note: this is *not a model answer*. Character points are indicated below in brief form, but students should (a) examine them to see whether they agree or disagree with them, or if if they can add to them; (b) they should seek out quotations and references which illustrate the points made (if they agree) or support their own points (if they disagree or if they find other points).

ambition, but not for herself, for her husband=**unselfish**
courageous – see particularly after the murder of Duncan
determined – where does she indicate this? What is the most important occasion when she displays **determination**?
quick-witted – are there indications before the banquet scene that she thinks fast?
practical – look for two instances which are linked to her
courage in the speed and efficiency with which she acts
stamina – is this a character point? Should we say **perseverance** – in word and deed – and link it to **determination**?
loyalty – to her husband – look at incidents before and after the murder of Duncan
Remember to be relevant in your answer. **Cunning**, **devious**, **unscrupulous**, **hypocritical** (find examples where she is each or all of these) would not be included, since they are not qualities to be admired.
Could we say that Lady Macbeth is **resilient** – that she recovers quickly? And would you use the sleep-walking scene as evidence that she had a heart and conscience about the crimes which she and her husband have committed and which he is going on committing without confiding in her? Read, think, support by quotation or reference. Is she **imaginative? Strong? bold? attractive?**
Are there any moments in the play when she displays **humanity? compassion? sensitivity? concern for others?** Closely examine the scenes in which she appears.
2 Describe Macbeth's dealings with the witches. How far are they responsible for his subsequent actions?
3 Indicate, with appropriate quotations, the main aspects of

Macbeth's character (a) up to and just after the murder of Duncan and (b) during the rest of the play.

4 How far does Macbeth's own imagination contribute to his downfall?

5 Compare Macbeth as a man with (a) Duncan; (b) Banquo; (c) Macduff.

6 Give an account of Macbeth's attitude towards (a) loyalty; (b) the life to come; (c) sleep; (d) life; (e) each of the witches' prophecies.

7 What do we learn of Macbeth from any *two* or *three* of his soliloquies, each taken from a different part of the play?

8 Examine the effect of light and dark images in the play, saying how they are related to the supernatural, the unnatural and the natural events in *Macbeth*.

9 How far can Lady Macbeth be held responsible for her husband's actions (a) before and (b) after the murder of Duncan?

10 How far is Lady Macbeth's assessment of her husband's character (Act I, Scene 5) accurate? You should refer to his actions after this.

11 As the play unfolds, the roles of Macbeth and Lady Macbeth are reversed. How far would you agree with this judgement?

12 Analyse the part played by *conscience* in Macbeth and Lady Macbeth.

13 Comment on Shakespeare's use of prose (a) in Macbeth's letter to Lady Macbeth; (b) in the Porter's scene; (c) in the murder of Lady Macduff and her son; (d) in the sleep-walking scene.

14 Write an extended essay on Shakespeare's use of *dramatic irony* in Macbeth.

15 Compare and contrast the effect on Macbeth of the visions of the dagger and the ghost of Banquo.

16 Give an account of the part played by the witches in *Macbeth*. Which is their most important scene and why?

17 Compare and contrast Malcolm and Macduff. Do you consider that either has any weakness of character?

18 Write an account of the scene you find (a) the most pathetic or (b) the most moving or (c) the most violent or (d) the most revealing, in each case supporting your answer by close reference to the text.

19 Write an essay on the use of *one* or *two* images in the play.

Shakespeare's art in *Macbeth*
Setting and themes

Setting

The action of *Macbeth* takes place nominally in 11th-century Scotland, but we are never very far from the sights and sounds that Shakespeare knew. For example, the description of Macbeth's castle in Inverness in Act I, Scene 6 could be of any castle known to Shakespeare, and perhaps in his native Warwickshire. Most of the Jacobean audience watching the play would have been to fairs where 'rarer monsters' were 'painted upon a pole' and, in an age that indulged in bear-baiting, would certainly be familiar with Macbeth's image of himself as a bear tied to a stake.

Themes

The main theme of *Macbeth* is aptly summarized in Macbeth's own words. He possesses

Vaulting ambition, which o'erleaps itself
And falls on the other. (Act I, Scene 7)

The real driving force behind that ambition is Lady Macbeth's; she urges him on when he expresses doubt and indeed completes the first crime herself. But the theme of ambition is related to all the other themes of the play, which include violence, tyranny, insecurity, evil, goodness, love and the supernatural. Hypocrisy and deception are obviously central to the main action; consequences, retribution are the results of that main action.

The characters

Macbeth

> Stars, hide your fires,
> Let not night see my black and deep desires.

Macbeth is dominated by the protagonist who gives the play its title. Initially he is seen as a great soldier, a fearless fighter who has loyally defended his king against a treacherous rebellion. However, he is corrupted by evil in the form of the witches and their supernatural evocations on the one hand, and by ambition, not so much his own at first but Lady Macbeth's ambition for him, on the other. Her strength motivates his actions; once begun, however, he realizes there is no going back, and he is forced to continue on his bloody path. *Impressionable*, he is easily influenced by the witches prophecies, the first of which is not a prophecy but a fact (he is already Thane of Glamis); the second is quickly proved accurate (he is made Thane of Cawdor by Duncan); while the third – that he will be 'King hereafter' – touches those wishes for kingship already existing in his subconscious. Yet he resists; he resists because he knows that he is abusing his better nature by entertaining the presence of murderous thoughts.

Shakespeare's psychological analysis of Macbeth's mind and emotions is both subtle and immediate, and its dramatic effect is achieved primarily through the use of soliloquies that reveal these inner workings. Macbeth is *imaginative, susceptible* and, as action follows action, increasingly *violent*; but his conscience, both before and after the murder of Duncan, is not completely stilled. His initial reactions to the murder are hysterical yet impotent showing that he realizes the enormity of his offence – against God, against humanity and against himself. A further manifestation of conscience can be seen in the terrible dreams, the immediate knowledge that he has 'murdered Sleep'.

Lady Macbeth's actions to cover her husband's *weakness* – she takes the daggers back to the room, and later faints or pretends to faint when she hears him say that he has killed the grooms – reflect the fact that her own estimate of her husband's character 'It is too full o' the milk of human-kindness/To catch the nearest way' is accurate. But what we are shown during the course of *Macbeth* is the transformation of the leading character from ambitious soldier to *tyrant* to *butcher* by the direct process of action; killing Banquo, then having Lady Macduff and her children killed, demonstrates Macbeth's terrible *insecurity*.

That insecurity is present from the beginning, and is seen in close-up, verbal rather than visual, as Shakespeare conveys the movements of self-debate before the actual murder of Duncan:

If it were done, when 'tis done, then 'twere well
It were done quickly . . . (Act I, Scene 7)

The hallucination of the dagger (Act II, Scene 1) shows how Macbeth is tempted (it illustrates too the vivid quality of his imagination), the swiftness of killing being something he has done on the battlefield but without moral or spiritual conflicts or consequences. As we have seen, consequences catch up with Macbeth as soon as the deed is done; he thinks he has heard voices saying that he has murdered sleep (ironically he has done so, for himself and, much later, for his wife) and he knows that he has sacrificed his soul to the devil. From then on he grows in evil practice and stature; firstly, his unwise killing of the guards arouses suspicion against him and, because of the danger to themselves (from Macbeth) Malcolm and Donalbain flee. Macbeth's immediate *remorse* after the murder of Duncan gives way here to his practical nature – he prepares, from now on, for any eventuality, and this disposal of the guards is his first step towards securing himself.

He is *superstitious* – witness his reactions to the witches – and this is further underlined as he tries to ensure that the third prophecy (that Banquo's heirs will be kings) does not come true. He cunningly questions Banquo about his and Fleance's movements before the feast; he delegates hired murders to kill them, having poisoned their already poisoned minds against Banquo, then is shaken into further hallucination and unguarded mutterings after he learns that Fleance has escaped. The banquet scene, with the ghost of Banquo appearing only to him, shows his deep-seated *fear*; it also shows the dramatist's fine symbolic 'placing', since the ghost sits in Macbeth's place at the banquet, and his heirs will ultimately occupy Macbeth's usurped place – the throne.

With the killing of Banquo Macbeth becomes more independent of his wife. He tells her to be 'innocent of the knowledge, dearest chuck/Til thou applaud the deed'. Now Macbeth takes responsibility for his deeds, and his determination to sustain his power at all costs, is shown in his assertion to Lady Macbeth that 'There's not a one of them, but in his house/I keep a servant fee'd.' Yet this freeing of himself from dependence on his wife is balanced by an increasing dependence on the witches. He determines to see them in order to be reassured, seeking supernatural aid to enforce his tyranny; thus he acknowledges their power and his own *corruption* – they are subserving the Black Arts of the Devil and fight 'Against the Churches', so that Macbeth has sold himself to evil. Their prophecies (Act IV, Scene 1) about Macduff, Birnam Wood coming to Dunsinane, and that none of woman born shall harm him, show Macbeth alternately fearful and reassured, though the appearance of Banquo and the eight kings unleashes his rage. His practicality now takes a completely *unscrupulous* turn, for he has Lady Macduff and her children murdered, again shying away from the actual deed himself.

Macbeth is off-stage for the rest of Act IV, but he lives vividly in the minds of audience and reader as Malcolm and Macduff talk graphically of the state of Scotland, and Ross reports the murder of his family to Macduff. The sleepwalking scene (Act V, Scene 1) further stresses Macbeth's distance from his wife, whose conscience has surfaced in madness while Macbeth's has sunk forever with each bloody crime. He has chosen to neglect his once 'dearest partner of greatness', ignore the disaffection among his troops, and cling to the infallibility of the witches, not realizing until his battlefield confrontation with Macduff, that their enigmatic statements have been double-talk, double-crossing him, their devious practices paralleling his own double-dealings.

In Act V Scene 5, with the news of Lady Macbeth's suicide and with wholesale desertion about him, Macbeth's reactions, though self-pitying, reveal the goodness that might-have-been and, such is Shakespeare's unerring focus on the inner man through soliloquy, the reader is moved to some compassion too. His pathetic wish for a happy and honourable old age is a genuine *self-recognition* of what he has denied himself, just as earlier (Act V, Scene 3) his urging of the doctor to purge or cleanse Lady Macbeth of her mental sickness carries within it an oblique acknowledgement of his own. Critics who have noted a lack of feeling in Macbeth do him scant justice; it is not lack of feeling, rather it is a tacit recognition that he *cannot change*, that after the first crime he is so set on a path of destruction and *self-destruction* that there is no going back. He recognizes that his actions are responsible for his wife's condition, and again we become aware of the subtlety of Shakespeare's psychological portrayal of characters.

The doctor's words that a mentally ill patient 'Must minister to himself' strike home to Macbeth, for he has not become too insensitive to realize that the words apply to him, and that he can do nothing about them except flee from himself into battle. Macbeth's reactions to his wife's death have been seen as callous; this is far from the truth. For him now there is only the stretching forward of meaningless, monotonous time, and life is a mockery. In a curious way, his fine lines 'Tomorrow, and tomorrow, and tomorrow' are an oblique looking back; the future holds nothing, the past held much, and his dead wife was part of that past.

When the Messenger brings the news that 'The wood began to move' Macbeth realizes that he is in the power of 'the fiend/That lies like truth' and resorts to the only certainty he knows, the certainty of fighting (and dying) like a soldier. Still he clings tenaciously to the other prophecy (though one has just been proved false), slays young Siward, fears capture, rejects suicide, learns that Macduff was from his mother's womb 'untimely ripp'd', curses the witches, and dies bravely, hopelessly (his death-wish very much evident). There is no tragedy in Macbeth's death; we have seen the tragedy played out in the character and actions of the man.

The character of Macbeth, like the play itself, is well and economically conceived. The inner man is revealed to us through the movements of temptation, partial rejection of that temptation, anguished reaction after the murder of Duncan, swift and impetuous and unscrupulous action thereafter, and a frightening descent beyond all personal redemption. Yet such is Shakespeare's greatness, seen here in the creation of this monstrous character, that Macbeth's soliloquies, his battle with himself, even his invocations to evil, are full of humanity; the vacillations, indecisions and unlicensed thoughts we all know in ourselves. His thoughts and emotional debates should be thoroughly studied, for every step in his anti-progress is carefully and psychologically integrated into his actions, Appearing strong and acquiring reputation, Macbeth is yet weak; his strength is physical, his weakness mental, emotional, moral. Every facet of the character is exposed to our view, largely through the character himself.

Any study of Macbeth's character must take account of the language he uses – night, darkness, blood – but balanced, to underline his moral and emotional struggle, by references to God and religion and damnation. No single term can define the full quality of his character, except to say that the embryo of evil within him becomes a monstrous and cancerous birth, growing and spreading throughout the whole personality. With sure insight, Shakespeare has identified and personalized in the character of Macbeth the coercive and enslaving power of evil. Men who become monsters are inhuman *and* pathetic, for they have denied humanity. Macbeth is there for all time, preserved in the living language of Shakespeare's truth.

Lady Macbeth

> These deeds must not be thought
> After these ways: so it will make us mad.

There could hardly be a more successful pairing, in terms of dramatic contrast and effect, than that of Macbeth and Lady Macbeth, who complement each other at every turn and twist of their minds, schemes and action. In the presentation of the Macbeths, Shakespeare uses a familiar and often subtly dramatic *motif*; the difference between what appears to be and what is. Thus Macbeth appears strong; he is often weak; Lady Macbeth appears a 'kind hostess'; she is a scheming and unscrupulous woman. Macbeth appears to be in command of himself; he is not; Lady Macbeth appears frightened when she thinks Macbeth may have failed to kill Duncan: she is soon self-possessed; takes the daggers back, smears blood on the grooms, and says, with long-term injury to herself, 'A little water clears us of this deed' (Act II, Scene 2). But if we ignore this *motif* for the moment, we note at once, in Lady Macbeth's reactions after she has read her husband's letter, that we are in the presence of a *strong, vital, determined* woman, ambitious for her husband, breathing exultation at the promise – which she will see is translated into fact – that her husband's present triumph will lead him to the throne. Her own assessment of her husband's character (Act II Scene 3, 16–25) is a masterly summary of what he is, and what we shall see he is. Her *will* is *uncompromising*, for straightaway she realizes that if he is to become king he must listen to her, be motivated by her *courage*; she indulges a terrible and ecstatic invocation to the evil spirits – the spirits that have set her husband's mind in motion – to keep in abeyance her womanly reactions and to fill her with 'direst cruelty', all this within the space of a few minutes after receiving her husband's letter.

By a subtle linking on Shakespeare's part, it is almost as if Lady Macbeth, like her husband, has had her subconscious thoughts sounded, and that they are now brought forward into her conscious mind as Macbeth's were by the prophecies. She is ecstatic in her feverishly emotional greeting of Macbeth, and follows this by taking full *responsibility* for the planning, perhaps even the coming execution, of the murder of Duncan. She also reveals her *cunning*, their joint need to be devious, when she tells her husband to 'look like th' innocent flower,/But be the serpent under't' (Act I Scene 5), the first overt note of the appearance/ reality, deception/truth theme which runs throughout the rest of the play. Her *hypocrisy* of course subserves this theme, with her ironic use of the word 'double' (echoed elsewhere several times in the play) informing her carefully rehearsed speech to Duncan in her role of 'honour'd hostess'. This outward show conceals a *passionate* and *unscrupulous* nature, which is brought fully into play when her husband says that he will not go on with the plan to murder Duncan. Her response, to call him a coward and to stress his impotence at the prospect of this action, shows the calibre of the woman, given a terrible and savage stress in her remembrance of having given suck to her child but being pre- pared to dash its brains out if she had been committed to murder Duncan as her husband assuredly is (Act I, Scene 7). This vivid picture, in all its vicious power and assertion, shows how completely Lady Macbeth has forced herself to become dehumanized in pursuance of ambition for her husband. She reveals her *practical* nature, outlining to her husband the details of the plan – to get the chamberlains drunk, murder Duncan, and then lay the blame on his 'spongy officers'. Such is the power of her personality, the persuasiveness of her language and the commonsense confidence she generates, that Macbeth responds positively, no longer hesitating to act.

At this stage Lady Macbeth is the stronger partner, manipu- lating her husband; thus the first act of *Macbeth* ends on a high if evil note, the woman directing the man's destiny. (The balance is to be ironically adjusted later when, having obtained that destiny for him, she herself becomes mad from the excesses of his actions and the insistent memory of her own.) She further shows her practical capacity for action when she drugs the grooms as she had promised, thus preparing the way for Macbeth's killing of Duncan without fear of detection. Yet, like Macbeth, she shows unexpected moments of humanity; she has set the dag- gers ready for Macbeth, and obviously thought of killing Dun- can herself, but was restrained because he resembled 'My father as he slept'. It is the merest chink in her emotional armour, for when Macbeth, obviously distracted by the enormity of his action, reappears, she has to summon both her fortitude and her reason in order to calm him down, keep him sane and complete the night's work. And here we see what a remarkable woman she is, having a stronger stomach for what has been done and what is still to do than her husband, who has had to prove himself many times on the battlefield. Her replies to his fearful, anguished near-hysteria, are brief, sensible, to the point, and even include the unconsciously prophetic and ironic remark included at the head of this character-study of her ('These deeds . . . it will make us mad' – Act II, Scene 2). In her case – and perhaps too in Macbeth's – her own prophecy comes tragically true. But her practical, down-to-earth nature, contrasted with the vivid and dislocated imaginings of her husband, urges her to get water to wash away the blood and, in direct counterpoint to her husband's present squeamishness, she takes the daggers and smears the guards with blood. Again she berates Macbeth for cowardice, refuses to be panicked by the knocking, suggesting that they both put on dressing-gowns to make it appear as if they have just got up. She is in *complete command*, both of herself and her husband; the result is that though he has done the deed she, in *calm competence*, has made sure that no guilt can attach to him.

With the scene of discovery upon them, Macbeth lives up to his public image as a man of action; Lady Macbeth, initially in control, exclaims in horror that Duncan should have been killed: 'What! in our house?', a brilliant indication of the shame that she is affecting to feel and of the disgrace for her and for Macbeth that it should have happened there. Knowing that the deed has been done, we feel the force of the dramatic irony in this utterance. But crisis is truly upon her, for Macbeth has jeopardized their plans by killing Duncan's attendants who, he reasoned to himself, would have denied that they had killed Duncan. Lady Macbeth realizes at once what a blunder this is, but whether she faints from shocked dismay, or feigns her faint in an improvised attempt to draw attention away from Macbeth, is uncertain. We know that she can act a part – we have seen her reception of Duncan – but real or feigned, this is a dramatic moment and may even indicate her guilt to those present.

From then on, Lady Macbeth's appearances are infrequent but important; she is seen before the murder of Banquo, and it is obvious that she too is feeling dissatisfied that what she and Macbeth have done may be ultimately for Banquo's descendants. But she is *supportive* and comforting to Macbeth, insisting that 'what's done is done' and that there is no point in brooding on it. This again shows her firmness; so far she is not bothered by her conscience, but she is aware of Macbeth's capacity for analysis, and of his insecurity. Lady Macbeth is not merely an accomplished hostess; she is also cunningly diplomatic, urging Macbeth to be charming to his guests at the banquet, knowing that he must try to allay any suspicions of himself by his 'appearance' if they are to conceal the terrible 'reality' of their guilt. But Macbeth, beset by fears, conceals another terrible 'reality' from her, the planned murder of Banquo. We might consider whether Lady Macbeth's strength has in fact been too strong for her husband, who, now that he is King, has pride and determination enough to act on his own. But again, in crisis, she acts practically and skilfully, doing all that is required and repairing as best she can the damage of what is unexpected, embarrassing and revealing. She urges her husband to control himself at the banquet after he has seen the murderers at the side door, and her *presence of mind* and *quick-thinking* enable her to account for Macbeth's strange behaviour when he, and he alone, sees the ghost of Banquo sitting in his place. 'My Lord is often thus' she says in extenuation of his distraction, and she further elaborates upon this by explaining to the nobles that if they take any notice of his behviour they will offend him. This is not only quick, it is a stroke of bold ingenuity, and shows that she is still strong-nerved, resilient, able to handle a crisis. Aside, she calls Macbeth a coward, reminds him of his other hallucination about the dagger, and even copes with Macbeth's guilty revelations by trying to steer him back to his duties towards his guests. But she cannot cope with the rooted, fixed obsession in his mind, for when he mentions Banquo – twice – the ghost appears to his tormented vision. Lady Macbeth still has the self-control to explain as best she can to the guests that her husband suffers from this disorder habitually, but when Ross asks an embarrassing question ('What sights, my Lord?') she is forced to get rid of the company without ceremony. Again we note her exceptional *poise*, but when everyone has gone she seems, judging from her brief remarks to Macbeth, to be exhausted by the events.

Lady Macbeth is now aware of the nature of her husband's disease, urges him to sleep and effectively disappears from the main current of the play's action thereafter. Macbeth is 'in blood/Stepp'd in so far' that she no longer has any direct influence on what he does. She is now, off-stage, the unequal

wife not the equal partner, aware or half-aware of what is happening, driven mad by the past and the present. Her absence
from Act IV marks the off-stage development of her madness,
but at the beginning of Act V we witness the effects of her
subconscious reactions in the sleep-walking scene. Her awareness of the enormities of their crimes is shown in the writing of
the letter while asleep. Is her subconscious fashioning a confession, a warning to Lady Macduff, or even an appeal to her
husband? We shall never know, but the dramatic impact is
immediate, poignant, tense. That active mind, so quick and
competent in action and response, is wrapped in the darkness of
insanity; events, and her own part in them, have distracted her
reason. She exists in the present, but her imagination lives in the
past. Her last sane words to her husband, 'You lack the season of
all natures, sleep' now ironically apply to her. The light she
keeps always beside her shows her fear of the darkness, (darkness symbolizes evil in the play) which was the cover for her own
evil deeds. 'The little water' can now never be enough to cleanse
either her hands or her soul – with splendid irony Shakespeare
invests her in her madness with her husband's capacity for
hallucination.

Her ramblings also embrace the murder of Lady Macduff
('The Thane of Fife had a wife: where is she now?') and the
traumas of the banquet scene. Others show her comforting her
husband while, again with irony, her firm-set, assured 'What's
done cannot be undone' is here picked up by her and repeated
in her brokenness. Nothing can be undone, but her poor shattered mind is the irrevocable result of the doing. Lady Macbeth
is one of the greatest dramatically realized characters in our
literature – callous, unscrupulous, bold, brave, quick-thinking,
strong, impulsive, impassioned, thinking more for her husband
and of him than she does of herself. But she is reduced and
battered by their deeds, and the retribution of conscience, which
she despised in Macbeth, eventually drives her insane. She later
kills herself, unable to remove the 'damned spot' or to 'sweeten
this little hand' which had taken the daggers, smeared them with
blood, and placed them beside the attendants of the murdered
king. Her man's heart in a woman's body sustains her while she
is in command of her husband who, later, pursues his ever more
bloody ends without admitting her to his confidence.

Duncan

The two major characters of *Macbeth* absorb our interest, but the other characters reflect patterns of parallel, contrast and opposition to them. Duncan is sufficiently contrasted with Macbeth to have more than a passing individuality; his appearances are brief but telling. His praise of Macbeth is heartfelt, and, by an underlining of his own main characteristic he uses the word 'honour' on a few occasions – in praise of the loyalty of the wounded Captain and, with unintentional irony, in praise of Lady Macbeth. During the reports of the battle scene (Act I, Scene 2) he shows a quickness of sympathy in his concern for the Captain. He also has the ability to make snap decisions, as when he tells Ross to go and inform Macbeth that he (Duncan) has appointed him Thane of Cawdor. Duncan is himself trusting and honourable; he set great store by the character of the previous Thane of Cawdor just as, in ironic parallel, he sets great store by the character of the Thane of Cawdor he has just appointed, and who is to betray him rather more successfully than did the previous one.

Duncan is a combination of humility, generosity and strength. He wishes he could thank Lady Macbeth more than he is able to, sends her a diamond in recognition of her reception of him, is moved to tears of happiness as he greets Macbeth and Banquo. He accords Banquo equal measure of praise with Macbeth (and perhaps this is a subtly diplomatic balancing of the two), but he is firm, decisive and open in announcing that his son Malcolm will be his heir. It is this winning honesty, a freedom from intrigue – in a play in which intrigue is to be one of the major themes – which establishes Duncan as a moral focus before his murder. His decision to stay at Macbeth's castle shows that his trusting nature, already exposed by the treachery of the previous Thane of Cawdor, is still the mainspring of his action. As he talks with Banquo while Macbeth broods on the naming of the 'Prince of Cumberland' Duncan continues to praise Macbeth and to delight in his achievements.

Duncan's appears to be a spiritual as well as a royal presence, as if he is conscious that spiritual and state responsibilities are one and the same thing. His last action in the play on stage is to kiss Lady Macbeth's cheek, a finely ironic touch by Shakespeare, since his 'honoured hostess' has already given him, by her covert instigation of her husband, what is really the kiss of death. Before that murder Duncan is ever present in Macbeth's mind for, in trying to persuade himself not to go through with the killing, he enumerates Duncan's many virtues; his meekness and humility, his unstained character and the fairness of his rule; for a moment, such is Duncan's influence, we feel that some of these virtues may have rubbed off on Macbeth.

Banquo

Banquo also serves as a contrast to Macbeth and, with a subtle variation, to Duncan; like Duncan's, his dramatic life is short. Reports of him in battle show that he was brave and loyal, though not perhaps possessing the strength or what would today be called the charisma of Macbeth. It is noticeable that Banquo addresses the witches, though they do not address him until he asks them to: it is as if he is tackling evil face to face. He is keen, observant, and has an immediate insight into Macbeth's reactions to the prophecies, noting both the starting and 'fear' in his initial response. He is fearless, speaking to the witches as one who does not fear 'Your favours nor your hate'. When they have vanished after their prophecies, Banquo voices doubts of their existence, but concedes that the Devil may 'speak true' when Ross announces that Macbeth has been made Thane of Cawdor; he is apparently not jealous of the fact that Ross greets Macbeth but not him.

Banquo's wisdom and judgement are apparent when Macbeth questions him about the prophecies; he asserts that the agents of evil begin with easy promises but that later they will betray, and deeply, whoever listens to them. He notes Macbeth's hopes for the crown, but at this stage foul play has not entered Banquo's mind. He is astute and certainly ponders on what has been said, though he is obviously sceptical; he notices Macbeth's self-absorption, and agrees to speak with him further about the witches. Greeted by Duncan, he is modest in his expression of loyalty, but when he talks with him at Macbeth's castle he reveals that, like Duncan, he is something of a nature lover – in itself an implication of Banquo's natural, uncomplicated and loyal character. This contrasts strongly with his mood on the night of the murder, for his sense of oppressiveness is itself a foreboding of evil. And this is where the subtle variation in the character contrast with Macbeth begins. It is a master-stroke by Shakespeare in the economic creation of character depth in Banquo; fearing temptation as he sleeps, and obviously associating that temptation with the witches, Banquo invokes the 'merciful Powers' – the good angels – to restrain his evil thoughts. For a moment we feel that he, like Macbeth, is tempted, but instead of yielding to the 'horrid image' he prays to be delivered from it. When he meets Macbeth he admits, such is his honesty, that he has dreamed of the witches, adding 'To you they have show'd some truth'. It is probable that Banquo himself hopes they will show him 'some truth' too. When Macbeth tells him that they will discuss the witches later and that it 'shall make honour for you' Banquo's reply is admirable in its integrity and directness. As A. C. Bradley rightly observes in his *Shakespearean Tragedy* (pp. 383–4). 'Banquo fears a treasonable proposal' from Macbeth, and by saying that he will keep 'My bosom franchised and allegiance clear' he is rejecting it in advance, implying that he will only accept 'honours' from Macbeth if there is no foul play, only 'honourable' behaviour.

Banquo arrives after the exit of Macduff and Lennox following the discovery of Duncan's murder; intially incredulous, he becomes suspicious after he has heard Macbeth's explanation of why he killed the grooms. Later he is to give these suspicions fuller expression, but here he stands unequivocally against 'treasonous malice' and is already questioning what he calls 'this most bloody piece of work'. His soliloquy at the beginning of Act III is equally uncompromising, for he says of Macbeth's election to the throne 'Thou play'dst most foully for't'. There is, however, a marked element of self-interest as well, for he hopes that as the witches have been proved right in Macbeth's case, they may also prove to be right in his. Banquo is somewhat naive when questioned about his and Fleance's movements, though he also echoes Macbeth's previous assertion of loyalty to Duncan when he says that his duties to Macbeth 'Are with a most indissoluble tie/For ever knit'. It is a cunning ambiguity, for it refers not only to the fact that Macbeth is king now, but to the 'indissoluble' secret they both share, the prophecies of the witches.

Macduff

After his brief indulgence of the Porter, Macduff proves to be a most positive character; his announcement of the discovery of Duncan's murder is put in extreme language, which emphasizes the horror, the sin, and mingling religious reference with the idea of the Divine Right of Kings (an idea embraced by James I and thus topical too). So overwrought is Macduff that he tries to find the right image to describe revulsion, referring to the Gorgon (which turned men to stone if they looked directly at it) and then to Doomsday. He is considerate to Lady Macbeth, but reveals the news to Banquo in the same breath, a mark of his righteous emotion and disgust. His suspicion of Macbeth is immediate, shown by his own question 'Wherefore did you so?' when Macbeth reveals that he has killed Duncan's attendants. Thereafter, and particularly in the next scene (Act II Scene 4), his words are charged with innuendo, implying that 'Those that Macbeth hath slain' and that Malcolm and Donalbain being suspected of 'the deed' are not truths but rumours convenient to Macbeth.

His inward thoughts are perhaps best demonstrated by his decision not to go to Scone for Macbeth's coronation, (a brave and independent stroke that ultimately brings the tyrant down upon Macduff's family). Matters are made worse when he obviously also refuses to attend Macbeth's banquet; Lennox reports that refusal as well as revealing that Macduff has gone to England to pray for assistance from the 'holy King', whose influence and piety contrast effectively – and ironically – with that of the 'unholy King' whom Macduff has rejected. If Macbeth is the agent of evil and night, Macduff is the agent of goodness and light, but not before he has experienced the most terrible and poignant suffering. It is one of the most moving and heart-rending moments in the play when Lady Macduff and her child are slain by Macbeth's hirelings, made all the more agonizing by Lady Macduff's doubts about her husband – and the whole tenor of the scene makes us doubt him too. But if Macduff is in error, if he really intends to put country before family, or if he feels that his 'dam' and 'pretty ones' are at least safe from Macbeth, then he pays a grievous price. As he talks with Malcolm in the King's palace in England he asserts his loyalty, urging strong action upon Malcolm, who in turn puts Macduff to the test, considering that he would not have left his wife and child unless he were in league with Macbeth. Macduff's response to Malcolm's (false) account of his own tyranny and lust verges on a far too tolerant loyalty when he says that the appointed King may have his fill of women and of lands and money, providing that he has other 'graces' to compensate. When Malcolm says that he has none of these, Macduff has the forthrightness and courage to say that Malcolm is 'not fit to live' and recalls that Duncan was 'a most Sainted King'. Malcolm reveals his true self, calling Macduff a 'child of integrity' and acclaiming his 'noble passion', but Macduff is thoughtful in reaction, needing time to weigh the conflicting things Malcolm has told him.

Rosse's delay in telling Macduff the news of his family's slaughter is moving dramatic irony, and also shows Macduff's concern on their account. Faced with the news Macduff blames himself, suffers anguish, but immediately thinks of revenge 'front to front' with Macbeth. Macduff represents loyalty at the expense of deep personal anguish, and although we may question his wisdom and judgement with regard to his family, there is no doubting his sincere attachment to his country, his unswerving determination to set things right, and his courage in refusing to be subservient to Macbeth's will.

Malcolm

Malcolm is sufficiently like his father Duncan, in an untutored way, though it is doubtful if Duncan would have been as devious in the testing of Macduff. Malcolm and his brother Donalbain, in their first reactions to their father's murder, reveal their fear and suspicions of Macbeth and decide to flee. Malcolm, in England, suspects treachery, hence his long exchange with Macduff in Act IV Scene 3. The main tenor of this is his determination to find out if Macbeth has bribed Macduff, and also to test Macduff's reactions to his own 'confession' that he (Malcolm) has worse vices and would be a worse tyrant than Macbeth. Malcolm speaks reverently of the 'good King' (Edward the Confessor), is greatly moved by Macduff's anguish when he learns that his family have been butchered, but immediately turns it to positive account by stressing the need for immediate action with their allies against Macbeth. The battle scenes show little of Malcolm, but he takes the crucial decision to make Birnam Wood 'move' towards Dunsinane, an action that probes Macbeth's deepest fears; there is every indication that Malcolm's organization of the attack – he is a leader despite his youth – is competent. His grief for the death of young Siward strikes us as genuine, and he creates the first Earls of Scotland, again indicating a concern, in part gratitude, for the exiled nobles who have fled from Macbeth's tyranny. We feel that wisdom and balance will be the marks of his rule; there is every promise that he will be his father's son in policy and in deed.

Minor characters

The other characters of *Macbeth* are virtually seen in passing, but bold strokes of dramatic immediacy bring them to life; witness the grief, anger and bitterness of *Lady Macduff* at her husband's leaving her and their family exposed to the vengeance of the tyrant, but also note her wit and resilience in reasoning and verbal quibbles with her son before their murder. *Rosse* is the messenger-cum-go-between, bringing news, always careful of his own safety, a time-server who will go along with whichever faction is in power or is likely to succeed. *Lennox* is much more the courtier who serves Macbeth but who, like Macduff, has strong suspicions of him; he bemoans the fate of Scotland, and determines on action to overthrow Macbeth. The *Old Man* acts as a symbolic, benevolent figure, wondering at the upheavals in nature, representing the 'goodness' of old age which Macbeth will never enjoy. *Siward* is a brave soldier, proud that his son died as he did, while the *Porter* is an excellent cameo of a garrulous, drunken type whose dramatic function is much more than his character; his verbal ingenuity and aggravating slow-ness indicate the range of Shakespeare's characterization. *The witches* are not characters but apparitions, existing in fact for their Jacobean audience and functionally dramatic for Macbeth and the reader. They symbolize the powers of evil; outward manifestations of the corruption that exists within human nature; the influence of the supernatural and the force of super-stition – initiators of false beliefs which carry tragic con-sequences. Their dramatic influence through the prophetic utterances is integral to the play.

Style and structure

Introduction

Macbeth is an economical play, the language subserving the main theme of evil and its components; temptation, corruption, murder, retribution. It is typical of the later plays, which have been called the mature tragedies, that the style is, to use a much worked critical maxim, 'words charged with meaning and associations'. In *Macbeth* these associations are of the essence; they set up resonances within the text that are picked up and repeated to convey the *irony* –and *dramatic irony* – of the action. The word 'blood', as one critic has noted, occurs over one hundred times in the play; this sufficiently shows the horrific nature of the action, which moves from the general killing of the reported battles to the specific killing of Duncan, Banquo, Lady Macduff and her children. Lady Macbeth kills herself and Macbeth is killed in battle by Macduff. Metaphorical language in all its force runs through the play, and Shakespeare's style, in this story of deception and murder, has both the variety and control to underpin his themes.

Imagery and symbols

Consider the *light* and *dark* imagery used by Macbeth and Lady Macbeth to express their motives and their deeds. Here, as elsewhere in *Macbeth*, Shakespeare uses all the elevation of *poetry* (and *Macbeth* is indeed a poetic play, though it is the poetry of terror and evil rather than the poetry of romance and love) to produce psychological and dramatic effects. Take Lady Macbeth's first invocation to darkness:

> Come, thick Night,
> And pall thee in the dunnest smoke of Hell,
> That my keen knife see not the wound it makes,
> Nor Heaven peep through the blanket of the dark,
> To cry, 'Hold, hold!' (Act I Scene 5)

This illustrates at once the richness, at times the terrible richness, of the language in *Macbeth*. Night equals evil, as does Hell, and darkness is necessary for the concealed carrying out of the deed. It cunningly anticipates the stabbing of Duncan (the blanket that covers him affords no protection in the darkness against the deed), and the cry anticipates the imaginary voice which Macbeth hears as he 'murders Sleep'. It thus encompasses, in its fine economy, the central action of the play, murder. But if this were all it would merely be a striking instance of condensed figurative power; however, it is echoed by Macbeth and later by Banquo. On the night of the murder Banquo, restless and fearful of his own 'cursed thoughts' observes that:

> There's husbandry in heaven;
> Their candles are all out. (Act II, Scene 1)

The darkness itself (here ironically equated with Heaven, but appropriate for the acts of Hell) provides the natural cover for the unnatural murder; Macbeth, in the same scene, refers to the fact that 'Nature seems dead' (as Duncan is soon to be) and also gently mentions 'The curtain'd sleep', which looks back by association to the 'blanket' image used by Lady Macbeth, and again evokes Duncan's chamber. The visual and symbolic echoes continue; in Act II, Scene 4 (Ross talking to the Old Man) we learn that light (nature, goodness, the sun, all representative of Duncan) has been shut out from the earth. Again the condensed force is remarkable; 'the heavens, as troubled with man's act', 'dark night strangles the travelling lamp' (the sun) and 'darkness does the face of the earth entomb/When living light should kiss it'. From Heaven/Hell/light/darkness we have been subtly moved to a wider, brief, profound suggestion. The association is with the crucifixion of Christ, when from the sixth to the ninth hour the sun was eclipsed and the earth covered in darkness. In the context of *Macbeth*, Duncan (goodness) has been crucified by the Macbeths (evil). Earlier, on the discovery of the murder, Macduff says;

> Most sacrilegious Murther hath broke ope
> The Lord's anointed Temple, and stole thence
> The life o'th' building! (Act II, Scene 3)

This is another Biblical, religious echo linked in tone to that of the crucifixion associations. We have examined these in some detail in order to demonstrate the chain of connected references set up in *Macbeth* by particular related images and statements; these should deepen our appreciation of the artistic and imaginative structure of the play. But we are not yet finished with darkness. As evil comes more completely into the ascendant, so the imagery and the action continue dark. Banquo is killed – the light is struck out factually and figuratively but, ironically, Fleance escapes into the darkness. Macbeth's invocation to evil before that is specifically to darkness – 'Come, seeling Night/Scarf up the tender eye of pitiful Day' (Act III, Scene 2) and, in the same scene,

Good things of Day begin to droop and drowse,
While Night's black agents to their preys do rouse.

His greeting to the witches in Act IV Scene 1 ('you secret, black and midnight hags!') is a further extension of his complete recognition of the evil courses he has embraced.

Most poignant of all in this sequence is Lady Macbeth's needing to have light constantly by her in her madness – before, so to speak, she puts out her own light by suicide. Her mind, though, is already in darkness: 'Hell is murky,' she says (Act V Scene 1) and this leads on to Macbeth's final 'Out, out brief candle!' (Act V, Scene 5), though this is yet another of the Biblical references that occur in the representations of light and darkness, life and evil, goodness and death. In *The Book of Job*, in the section significantly headed 'Anger is powerless against the course of Justice' we read

'The wicked man's light must certainly be put out,
his brilliant flame cease to shine,
In his tent the light is dimmed,
the lamp that shone on him is snuffed. (Job 18, 5–6)

And this is exactly what happens to Macbeth. Thus in the literal text of the play there is a sub-text of reference that enriches the reader's experience and enhances his appreciation, and which constitutes in part the greatness of the play, showing Shakespeare's wealth of knowledge and demonstrating how he put it to dramatic and artistic use.

Clothes

The alert reader of the play will probe other sequences of description and imagery, for example the '*clothes*' sequence, which begins with Macbeth's 'borrowed robes' and has its pivotal emphasis in Macduff's ironic 'Lest our old robes sit easier than our new' at the end of Act II. Here the implication is quite clear. Macbeth not only 'borrows' the robes of royalty, he wears them, yet in a sense they are only 'borrowed' for his corrupt period of office; and he knows from the prophecy that the 'robes' will not go to his descendants. The clothes imagery contributes markedly to the theme of appearance and reality.

Sleep

Consider also the description of *sleep*, so beautifully evoked by Macbeth in:

> the innocent Sleep;
> Sleep that knits up the ravell'd sleave of care,
> The death of each day's life, sore labour's bath,
> Balm of hurt minds, great Nature's second course,
> Chief nourisher in life's feast . . . (Act II, Scene 2)

This again reaches out into one of the major concerns of *Macbeth*; the relationship between conscience, action, and consequences. Here Macbeth realizes what he has done and later refers to the terrible dreams that 'shake us nightly'. 'Macbeth shall sleep no more' becomes a running if largely unvoiced element in the play, but again it has ironic connections; Lady Macbeth, become mad, is in the literal sense to sleep no more, her dreams of the terrible past – and present – manifesting themselves in her sleep-walking. Lack of sleep, terrible dreams, are obviously connected with the murders done during darkness.

The grave

Sleep has been equated with death, but it is also equated with the *grave*, and awareness of the grave is another strong element in *Macbeth*. Macbeth himself becomes obsessed, after he has seen Banquo's ghost, with the return of the spirits of those who have been murdered. Before that (Act III, Scene 2) he had pondered on death, almost envying the murdered King:

> Duncan is in his grave;
> After life's fitful fever he sleeps well;

After the ghost sits in his chair he is 'unmann'd and panics; this hallucination moves not so much his conscience as his fear:

> If charnel-houses and our graves must send
> Those that we bury back, our monuments
> Shall be the maws of kites. (Act III, Scene 4)

And this is emphasized later in the same scene when Macbeth's fear embraces the supernatural in chance discoveries of murder:

> It will have blood, they say: blood will have blood:
> Stones have been known to move, and trees to speak;
> Augurs, and understood relations, have

By magot-pies, and choughs, and rooks, brought forth
The secret'st man of blood.

This fear of exposure from beyond the grave sets Macbeth into a
frenzy of killing, eliminating all those who might expose him. So
ruthless and widespread are his actions that they cause Rosse to
use the image when he speaks of Scotland as:

Almost afraid to know itself. It cannot
Be call'd our mother, but our grave; (Act IV, Scene 3)

The natural and supernatural

One of the main strands of *Macbeth* is the way in which the
natural is linked with the *supernatural*. After the murder, in
addition to the darkness we have an account that includes the
mousing owl killing the hawk and of Duncan's horses eating
each other, unnatural parallels with 'the deed that's done'.
Nature itself represents goodness, seen in Duncan's reaction to
the natural beauty at Macbeth's castle, down to the natural habits
of the sand-martin. Description or images frequently have a
symbolic significance in *Macbeth*, and it is noteworthy that the
poetry of beauty or of peace, as we might expect in such a
sombre play, is rare compared with the rhetoric of violence or
evil that dominates the action. Lady Macbeth's invocations to
nature are bitter ('The raven himself is hoarse'), as are those to
herself ('Come to my woman's breasts/And take my milk for
gall'), while Macbeth's are usually violent. We have noted his
pathetic rhetoric on sleep, and before he is persuaded to undertake the murder of Duncan he uses terms like 'angels' and 'Pity,
like a naked new-born babe' and 'Cherubins', (*sic*) terms of
Christian sanctity and observance.

The witches

Once he has killed, the invocations are to those agents of evil, *the
witches*. The first scene of the play, as L. C. Knights has noted,
'strikes one dominant chord', and that chord is evil. 'Fair is foul,
and foul is fair' underlines the appearance/reality theme; what
appears fair – a prophecy, a hostess, a pleasant castle – conceals
what is foul: ambition without scruple; plots, deception, murderous acts. By a dramatic sleight of hand, Shakespeare has
Macbeth repeat these words, thus linking him indelibly with the
witches before he sees them. We have already noted the drama-

tic function of the witches, but we should look too at their place in the structure of the play. The light rhyming couplets of their incantations contrast with the heavy evil they are bent on conjuring in the mind of man. They sound the notes of superstition with their magic numbers, their ritual revolving around the number three. Strangely, Macbeth is directly involved in three specific murders, those of Duncan, Banquo, Lady Macduff and her family, while the witches' 'nine times nine' torture approximates, or anticipates, the extent of Macbeth's murders in Scotland.

The enigmatic or ambiguous nature of the witches' prophecies reflects the enigmatic nature of man himself, subject to evil actions or thoughts unless ruled by what is natural rather than unnatural. On a low level they represent the idea of fate, chance, superstition within man. Their 'honest trifles', as Banquo calls them, merely 'appear'; what is concealed (evil) is 'real'. Act IV Scene 1 is of a piece with these scenes, the cauldron incantation being singularly expressive, with its list of animal and fleshly parts as invocation, all peculiarly appropriate when we think of the final description of Macbeth as a 'butcher'. Moreover, the phrase 'Double, double toil and trouble', while it is definitive of Macbeth's state and actions, echoes as well the key word 'double', much used in the play to indicate extreme force or deception, and picked up by Macbeth in the same scene ('But yet I'll make assurance double sure').

Significantly, the show of eight kings is completed by a ninth apparition following, that of the 'blood-bolter'd Banquo', thus making up the magic number of nine. By a considered linking, therefore, Shakespeare has connected the natural, the supernatural and the unnatural.

Verse: couplets

We have briefly noticed the witches' rhyming lines; Shakespeare's control of a variety of blank verse techniques – and the heavier rhyming couplets for emphasis or to end scenes – makes for flexibility of utterance and effect, which covers the whole range from natural speech through rhetorical power to poetic exaltation. The use of the couplet at the end of a scene is not just casual employment of an established convention. Take the end of Act III, Scene 1:

It is concluded: Banquo, thy soul's flight,
If it find Heaven, must find it out tonight.

Again, the alert reader will remember another scene ending that anticipates this, and mirrors it in spirit:

Hear it not, Duncan; for it is a knell
That summons thee to Heaven, or to Hell (Act II, Scene 2)

Sometimes the rhyming couplet contains the play on words that we have previously noted elsewhere in this section. Ross says, in reply to Duncan's rhyming couplet making Macbeth Thane of Cawdor:

I'll see it done,
What he hath lost, noble Macbeth hath won. (Act I, Scene 2)

Key words

The words 'done', 'lost' and 'won' are key words in *Macbeth*. 'Lost' and 'won' are used by the second Witch, who is referring to the battle, but again used here in the following scene, evidence of the closeness of verbal texture in the play, the echoes setting up almost subliminal associations in the reader's mind. The battle is 'lost and won'; Cawdor loses his life, Macbeth wins his title but, ironically, loses his soul. He wins the crown but loses his wife and ultimately wins nothing but hate. 'Done' or words derived from it, essentially simple expressions, are much more prevalent in the text than the examples given above. These begin with Lady Macbeth's striking analysis of her husband's character after reading his letter (Act I, Scene 5); she echoes one of the words above ('yet would'st wrongly win'), then saying of Macbeth that he would have:

That which cries, 'Thus thou must do,' if thou have it;
And that which rather thou dost fear to do,
Than wished should be undone. (Act I, Scene 5)

The play on 'done' and 'undone' continues throughout the planning and murder sequences of the first three acts. Lady Macbeth gives pointed irony to the word by connecting it with 'double' which, as we have seen, has associations and innuendoes of its own, when she says to Duncan:

All our service,
In every point twice done and then done double . . . (Act I, Scene 6)

The next scene opens with a triple reference that we have already considered in relation to the characters of Macbeth but it is worth even closer examination here; the repetition of the word indicates the emotional pressures, and act as index to the mind of a man of action who is yet hesitating before an action which, in his heart, he knows to be wrong:

If it were done, when 'tis done, then 'twere well
It were done quickly: (Act I, Scene 7)

The technical achievement here is remarkable; in one and a half lines of blank verse there is rich psychological and verbal compression. But the simple word, standing for the major deed, is always to hand for Macbeth. When the bell rings which signals immediacy of action he says, 'I go, and it is done', almost as if the action is already accomplished; here the ironic overtone, the wish-fulfilment, is apparent. He does *do* the deed but the emotional ramifications are immediate and complex to himself; the accomplishment is far from simple since it sets up an hysterical reaction which he cannot contain.

The Old Man in Act II Scene 4 refers to the darkness after the murder as 'unnatural/Even like the deed that's done' but Lady Macbeth, seeking to prevent the onset of brooding in her husband, says comfortably to him (and this is before the murder of Banquo) 'what's done is done' (Act III, Scene 2); but by the end of the same scene, perhaps bewildered by his reactions and by his assertion that 'there shall be done/A deed of dreadful note' she asks 'What's to be done?'. The deed *is* done, but such is Macbeth's suspicion, and so wedded is he to the simple word of action that, when he sees the ghost of Banquo sitting in his place, he says 'Which of you have done this?' Lady Macbeth responds by saying 'When all's done/You look but on a stool'. Hecate also picks up the word ('All you have done/Hath been but for a wayward son').

Lady Macduff's first words (Act IV, Scene 2) about her husband, 'What had he done, to make him fly the land?' are pathetically reinforced by her saying twice 'I have done no harm' before her murder. The final mention is redolent of the poignancy of Lady Macbeth's madness; in her last words she says 'What's done cannot be undone' (Act V, Scene 1). It is almost the epilogue to the play itself. We have here focused on a simple word – doubtless another would have 'done' as well – in order to show the power and resonance of Shakespeare's language.

The soliloquy

One of the main dramatic and literary devices in the play is the use of the *soliloquy*, where one character is alone on stage – or

perhaps speaking to himself aside while others are present –
revealing his inner thoughts, reactions, motives, ideas. The soliloquy is the dramatic indicator of what may or may not happen
but, more than this, it establishes an intimacy between character
and audience/reader of the play. Both Macbeth and Lady Macbeth reveal themselves in their soliloquies, which are invariably
charged with meaning; the first uttered by Macbeth is a case in
point. It is an aside which runs to sixteen lines and these encap-
sulate Macbeth's own battle with good and evil. He has just
learned that he is Thane of Cawdor, but immediately feels those
stirrings of temptation ('Whose horrid image doth unfix my hair
. . . My thought, whose murder yet is but fantastical').

Lady Macbeth's first soliloquy is an analysis of her husband's
character, her ambition for him, and an expression of her own
power over him; but the second, which follows the announcement of Macbeth's imminent arrival, is impassioned rhetoric,
her own invocation to evil with its terrible emphasis on the
elimination of all womanly feelings. It shows at once her
potential, the dangerous influence she is going to exert, her
capacity to go to an extreme to achieve what she wants for her
husband. Thus far we have seen that the soliloquy reveals
character and motivation, and Macbeth's 'If it was done . . .'
referred to earlier in this section is the supreme example. The
see-sawing movement of the verse reflects the battle, and ultimately leads to his deciding 'We will proceed no further in this
business', only to be overcome by Lady Macbeth's unsparing
indictment. This soliloquy carries its own ironic message, for it
shows the man thinking what he will do; the fact that immediately afterwards he doesn't keep to what he has decided prepares us for the other weaknesses in his character to be revealed.

Other soliloquies which will repay close attention from the
student are given below. The hallucination with the dagger
marks another stage in Macbeth's development, his complete
surrender to the forces of evil. Here the mainspring is towards
action, thus escalating the dramatic tension. At the beginning of
the next scene we have Lady Macbeth's account of her own
boldness and the statement that 'He is about it'. Macbeth, alone,
prepares for, undertakes, the deed, while Lady Macbeth, alone,
knows that he is doing it; Macbeth's soliloquies increasingly
reveal the man who has grown away from his wife in thought
and deed.

At the beginning of Act III there is Banquo's important soliloquy. He reveals his suspicions of Macbeth ('Thou playd'st most

foully for't'), with 'foully' again echoing the 'fair is foul' theme. But it also reveals Banquo's hopes for his own descendants and therefore for himself and, adds another dimension to his character – the need for a kind of wish-fulfilment despite his integrity. And Banquo is the cause of another Macbeth soliloquy in the same scene, full of jealousy and vengeance: 'for Banquo's issue have I fil'd my mind'.At the end of Act IV, Scene 1 Macbeth's descent into even more unscrupulous, murderous tyranny is indicated when he tells the audience 'The castle of Macduff I will surprise . . . give to th'edge o'th'sword/ His wife, his babes.' For a terrible moment, so maniacal is his desire to eliminate any succession to the throne, he seems to have confused Macduff with Banquo, but we soon realize that he is now mad, demented, and will brook no opposition.

Variety

Shakespeare employs in *Macbeth* the language of everyday speech; the elevated or rhetorical language of poetry; the varied and broken blank verse lines to convey naturalness in dialogue, and also prose. It is a general truth in Shakespearian drama that verse distinguishes the characters of high or noble birth, prose being used for the lower orders. This applies to *Macbeth*, though in this play there is an extension in particular ironic ways. We have seen, for example, that the verse of the witches usually conveys a light, incantatory affect; the blank verse, however, is used for varied effects. Here the rhetoric can indicate heroic action:

For brave Macbeth (well he deserves that name),
Disdaining Fortune, with his brandished steel,
Which smok'd with bloody execution,
Like Valour's minion, carv'd out his passage,
Till he fac'd the slave . . . (Act I, Scene 2)

The personification of 'fortune' and 'Valour's minion' creates a larger-than-life image of Macbeth, and this is needed to make all the more complete his tragic fall from grace and, ironically, his 'Disdaining Fortune' in a bloody-minded and treacherous way.

Sometimes the tone can be conversational *and* poetic, as in the exchange between Duncan and Banquo outside Macbeth's castle:

Duncan   This castle hath a pleasant seat; the air
Nimbly and sweetly recommends itself
Unto our gentle senses.

> This guest of summer
> *Banquo* The temple-haunting martlet, does approve
> By his loved mansionry, that the heaven's breath
> Smells wooingly here: (Act I, Scene 6)

Natural conversation, but rich in references which contrast tellingly with the main images of the play; if you like, it is the last glimpse of what is essentially light and natural.

Prose

If the figurative language of *Macbeth* is rich in its variety, we should not ignore the variety and contrast in usage of the prose. The Porter's scene stands out, but we should also look at the quality of the prose in Macbeth's letter to Lady Macbeth (Act I, Scene 5), the prose exchange between Lady Macduff and her son, and the prose of the sleep-walking scene. Macbeth's letter to his wife sets in train the whole action of the play; it is an economical account of what has happened, some thirteen lines of succinct reportage, containing phrases like 'the perfect'st report', the echo of the witches' 'All-hail' in Duncan's 'all-hail me "Thane of Cawdor"' and the ironic 'my dearest partner of greatness', initially true of Lady Macbeth though not later on. The factual prose contrasts immediately with Lady Macbeth's poetic ecstasy as she moves from analysis to passionate utterance, seeing herself as the motivating and guiding factor in Macbeth's gaining the throne. In a sense, the letter also conveys Macbeth's dependence on his wife and, more importantly, the intimacy between them.

Act II, Scene 3, often called 'the Porter's scene' is a misnomer, since the porter actually appears in under half of it, the rest of the scene being devoted to the discovery of Duncan's murder, Macbeth's off-stage killing of the grooms, the reactions of half-a-dozen characters. It is a finely dramatic scene, the porter's delay serving to heighten suspense, with his bawdy, half-drunken innuendoes a kind of dramatic irony anyway. This delay comes after the haste, panic, and decision of the previous scene and thus contrasts with it, with its language of commonplace repetition at the same time carrying immediate connections with what has, unbeknown to the porter, just occurred. Practically, of course, remembering that this is a play, this delay gives time for Macbeth and Lady Macbeth to clean up, change and compose themselves.

The introduction of an ordinary man with whom they could identify would also please the groundlings. But the references to 'Hell-Gate', 'Belzebub', 'the farmer ... expectation of plenty', 'time-pleaser', 'equivocator' and 'treason enough' sufficiently indicate the closeness of Shakespeare's craftsmanship, his ability to relate everything in the play to everything else there, for this scene is integral to the play as a whole. The low character uses low and sometimes obscene language to mirror, distort, contrast, highlight the language of noble characters whose actions are low, obscene and distorted in their practice of regicide. The Porter does not know this; the author, and the audience, do. The porter's prose in its earthy and bawdy associations, suggests real low life but it also implicitly relates to the main actions of the play. The respite before discovery is not just tediously filled; it is relevant and diverse in its comments.

A mixture of blank verse and prose is found in the scene where Lady Macduff and her son are murdered. Her conversation with Rosse and initially with her son is in blank verse, and indeed, with its ironic wit, the teasing quality of question and answer, is in short, staccato half-lines which make for naturalness and reflects the unease in Lady Macduff's mind. The verse is a kind of free verse, which descends into prose as the climax of the scene – the entry of the Murderers – approaches. The joke is a forced joke that indicates fear and perhaps incipient hysteria as Lady Macduff talks her way through the bitterness she feels at the desertion of her husband. Her 'I can buy me twenty at any market' has a simulated flippancy which conceals the deep hurt; her acknowledgment that Macduff has behaved as a traitor – 'Ay, that he was' – is an overt statement of her deepest feelings. The banter with her son is a means of keeping her grief at bay, and the precocious reasoning of the boy, with its adult method, contains the underlying emphasis that traitors should be hanged, and that 'there are liars and swearers enow to beat the honest men', a comment on Macbeth's reign. The prose part of this scene conveys naturally the language and atmosphere of a mother talking to her child; it contrasts effectively with the higher-flown language of Rosse and the Messenger, who both make themselves scarce before the arrival of the Murderers.

The sleep-walking scene provides prose of a very different order. Reportage by the doctor and the gentlewoman is followed by the entrance of Lady Macbeth with a taper; the prose is used not only by the lower ranks of society but reflects at the same time Lady Macbeth's fall from 'noble' society as well as losing her nobility of reason. The prose in *Macbeth* provides an admirable contrast to the elevated poetry and, in fact, is one of the patterns of contrast that form the structure of the play.

Further reading

The Arden Shakespeare: Macbeth, Edited by Kenneth Muir (Methuen 1951, reprinted 1982). Read particularly the Introduction.

Shakespearian Tragedy, A. C. Bradley (Macmillan 1904, reprint 1952). Good chapter on *Macbeth*.

Explorations, L. C. Knights (Chatto & Windus 1946, Penguin 1964). Contains his essay on 'How many children had Lady Macbeth?'

Shakespeare's History Plays, E. M. W. Tillyard (Chatto & Windus 1944). Macbeth as an historical play.

Shakespeare Survey 19 (Cambridge University Press 1966). The annual volume of Shakespeare studies, this one devoted to *Macbeth*.

Pan study aids Selected titles published in the Brodie's Notes series

GCSE Coursework English Coursework: Drama & Poetry
  English Coursework: Prose

Jane Austen Emma Pride and Prejudice

Geoffrey Chaucer (parallel texts editions) The Nun's Priest's Tale
The Pardoner's Tale Prologue to the Canterbury Tales
The Wife of Bath's Tale

Gerald Cole Gregory's Girl

Charles Dickens David Copperfield Oliver Twist

George Eliot Silas Marner

E. M. Forster A Passage to India

William Golding Lord of the Flies

Graham Greene Brighton Rock

Thomas Hardy Far from the Madding Crowd
The Mayor of Casterbridge Tess of the d'Urbervilles

Susan Hill I'm the King of the Castle

Christopher Marlowe Doctor Faustus

George Orwell Animal Farm 1984

J. B. Priestley An Inspector Calls

William Shakespeare Antony and Cleopatra As You Like It
Coriolanus Hamlet Julius Caesar King Lear Macbeth
The Merchant of Venice A Midsummer Night's Dream Othello
Romeo and Juliet The Tempest Twelfth Night

John Steinbeck Of Mice and Men and The Pearl

Keith Waterhouse Billy Liar

John Webster The Duchess of Malfi